Facets of
COMMUNICATION 360°

Facets of
COMMUNICATION 360°

ANAND CHHABRA
AND VINOD MITRA

An imprint of Manjul Publishing House Pvt. Ltd.
• C-16, Sector 3, Noida, Uttar Pradesh 201 301, India
Website: www.manjulindia.com
Registered Office:
• 2nd Floor, Usha Preet Complex, 42 Malviya Nagar, Bhopal 462 003 – India
Distribution Centres
Ahmedabad, Bengaluru, Chennai, Hyderabad,
Kochi, Kolkata, Mumbai, Noida, Pune

Facets of Communication 360° by Anand Chhabra and Vinod Mitra

This paperback edition first published in India in 2025

ISBN 978-93-5543-784-6

Cover design: Sakshi Agarwal

Printed and bound in India by Repro India Limited.

Dedicated to Our Daughters
Shyamli & Bhavna

Contents

Foreword

When I think about the number of times I succeeded or stumbled, one factor consistently stands out: communication.

I learnt this trick back in my younger days of struggle. I understood that the only thing I needed to start doing was talk more, so I did. Soon, I was advised to listen more and talk less. When I started listening, people advised me to work on connecting skills. Soon, I played cascade, trying to keep all the balls in the air. With much help, I was able to understand and be satisfied.

The reason was simple, though I realised it quite late: Communication is not an isolated activity but a continuous process, like breathing. You communicate when you blink, wave, turn your face, put your hands in your pocket or land a punch on someone's face. Believe it or not, even silence is a form of communication.

The book you hold in your hand is more than just a guide—it's a journey into genuinely understanding what it means to communicate. Engaging stories and practical tips will reinforce the truth that our ability to listen, speak, and connect with others shapes everything from our closest relationships to our professional achievements.

I wish this book had appeared twenty-five years earlier for the older generations to have a guide to fall back on. *Facets of Communication 360°* approaches conversations and relationships in a wholesome manner, leaving you better equipped to navigate the complexities of modern communication.

Samar Vijay, entrepreneur, and
author of *A Tryst with Money*
and *In Control of Money*

The Basics

1

Communication 360°

TS Matthews, editor of *Time* magazine from 1949 to 1953, wrote:

> 'Communication is something so simple and difficult that we can never put it in simple words.'

Between the simplicities and complexities in communication are several shapes, designs, contours, and colours!

- Communication is verbal and non-verbal.
- Communication is one-to-one, one-to-few and one-to-many.
- Communication is social norms and behaviours.
- Communication is speaking, listening, saying NO and effective questioning.
- Communication is growing up, as well as friendships, fighting, anger, and love.
- Communication is travelling, sightseeing, visiting relations and attending marriages and functions.

- Communication is about the workplace, personal, social, and business.
- Communication is conflict and resolution, disputes and mediations, building a nation, destroying a culture, getting a tough bill passed in the parliament, political manoeuvrings, wars, and backroom negotiations.
- Communication is about influencing style—aggressive, submissive, and assertive.
- Communication is the key to leadership, teaching, training, and coaching.
- Communication is the building block for team building—about managing the environment at the workplace, at home, on the road and among friends.
- Communication is planning and project management.
- Communication is woven into social interactions—it's laughter, etiquettes, lively dinners, relaxed picnics, shared gossip, card parties, secrets, playful teasing, romance, and light-hearted banter.
- Communication is music, poetry, dance, drama, storytelling, love letters, books, movies, New Year greetings, good morning and WhatsApp messages, and graphics.
- Communication includes walkie-talkies, loudspeakers, megaphones, telephones, mobile phones, emails, videos, selfies, Facebook, LinkedIn, WhatsApp, YouTube Shorts, Instagram Reels, and Snap Chat.
- Communication is Holi, Diwali, Ram Lilas, Dusshera, Independence Day, Republic Day, Eid, Christmas, and New Year's Day.
- Communication is kite flying, music sabhas and concerts, singing and dancing in chaupals and melas.
- Communication involves morning prayers in schools, singing aarti and bhajans in temples, azaan from mosques, and choir service singing in churches.

- Communication is central to all activities around which the universe evolves and revolves.
- We share knowledge and experiences and exchange facts, ideas, opinions, and emotions to create mutual understanding. We influence and understand each other better to build relationships, delegate responsibilities, coordinate, manage a team, or meet social expectations.
- Communication is the foundation on which a family is built and functions.
- Communication is an excellent skill that enhances our performance—helping us do more, faster, and better continuously.
- Communication has given wings to imagination to help humans build a mighty civilisation, progress in every field, and continuously improve our lives and living conditions.

Let us embark on the journey of this beautiful and bewildering world of communication from a 360° perspective, examining its different facets.

2
Communication Defined

The sound—the basic element—started it all. A child's cries, hunger pangs, laughter, exhilaration, and contentment all existed in the universe. It transformed into communication when the mother understood her baby's language—initially non-verbal and later verbal and responded.

Communication is transferring information (a message) between two or more sides to understand and share their thoughts. Effective communication is a vital life skill, essential to delivering and understanding information quickly and accurately to achieve the desired outcome.

In its basic form, communication takes place between two participants:

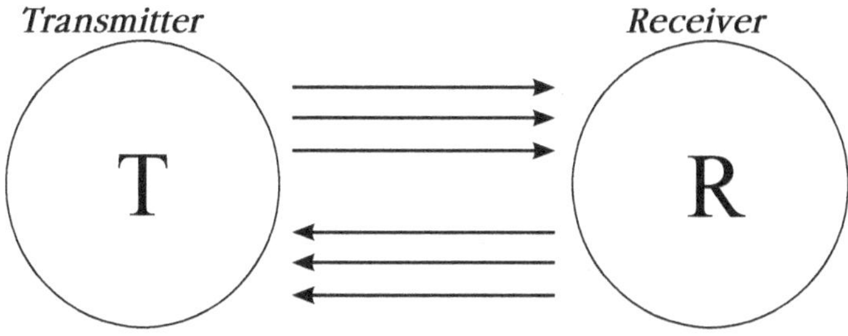

Transmission of a message between these two takes place in three distinct stages:

A. Communication starts with the Transmitter converting their thought into a message and forwarding it to the Receiver.

   However, the transmitter may be mentally or physically distracted while initiating the message. This phenomenon is generally described as a 'slip of the tongue'.

B. The next part is the journey from the Transmitter to the Receiver.

   Though we presume otherwise, several challenges—physical or otherwise—exist in the medium through which the message is passing, which may result in non-transmission or loss of the message's content in transmission. These disturbances, generally referred to as communication gaps, could be:

   - Physical impediments—fog, dust, clutter, noise, etc.
   - Distractions—visible and invisible.
   - Use of different languages, locations, emotions, and cultural backgrounds.
   - Stress among the two communicators.

- Absence of eye contact or body language.

These challenges may seriously affect its transmission as the message may not reach the Receiver, or the content may get distorted.

C. The third part is receiving the message at the Receiver's end.

In the first place, the Receiver should know that a message has been transmitted to him. He would then anticipate the arrival of the message. Otherwise, the message might get lost.

Next, the Receiver decodes the message by looking at its contents.

The mere arrival of the message at the Receiver's end does not complete the Communication. The Transmitter does not know whether the Receiver has received their message and whether the latter has received the contents in full.

If the transmitter gets a confirmation from the receiver about both events, that would be awesome. Otherwise, the Transmitter must either send the message again or try to reach out to the Receiver through other means.

This would imply that the Receiver must provide feedback to the Transmitter in two parts:

i. Confirm to the Transmitter that a message has been received, and
ii. The message's contents have been received.

Both these requirements will be fulfilled if the Receiver paraphrases what has been received. This may even provide him with an opportunity to seek further clarification.

The Transmitter closes the loop by clarifying, explaining, modifying, or providing additional information.

Thus, the RESPONSIBILITY & ACCOUNTABILITY for transmitting a message lies with the Transmitter.

As the dialogue progresses, they keep interchanging their roles from Receiver to Transmitter and Transmitter to Receiver.

In sum, communication is not a one-way but a two-way street, a dialogue.

So simple! Then why do we find effective communication a big challenge? Communication is the key to managing our environment effectively.

The complexity lies in its detailing and implementation of the essential communication principles.

Let us study communication in all its facets and unravel its nuances.

3

Verbal Communication

Verbal communication means sharing your views, information, feelings, thoughts, and ideas through sound and spoken words. It primarily includes oral communication, while written and visual communication are distinct forms of communication, which we will discuss separately.

Verbal communication can be divided into the following three broad categories:

1. *Interpersonal Communication*: One-on-one communication between two people, such as face-to-face and video conferencing.
2. *Small-Group Communication*: One-to-a-few communications such as office, team, sales, or board meetings; school sessions; press conferences; family gatherings; and video conferencing.
3. *Public Communication*: One-to-many (large audiences) communication includes public speaking, election meetings, campaigns, etc.

Verbal Communication

In face-to-face interactions, verbal communication may be accompanied by non-verbal communication. The broad differences between Verbal and Non-verbal communication are:

Category	Verbal Communication	Non-verbal Communication
Medium	The exchange of information is primarily oral, using voice.	Line of vision. Face-to-face interaction without the use of words.
Mode	Face-to-face communication, audio or video recordings, loudspeakers, etc.	Hand movements, facial expressions, eye movements, etc.
Decoding Level	Highly structured, formal, easy to understand and less confusing if the language used is common.	Unstructured, and informal, could be misinterpreted.
Awareness	Keen awareness as the speaker needs to think and analyse before speaking.	Involuntary on the part of the speaker. Keen awareness on the part of the listener.
Formality	More formal.	Less formal.

Effective Verbal Communication

To communicate effectively, the speaker must address two aspects: *'What to say'* and *'How to say'*.

'What to say' is the content of the message. A direct, accurate, complete, precise, and concise message will be accepted readily. The language used must be courteous and straightforward to avoid misinterpretation of the message. Against this, abusive or threatening comments involving attire, background, family, culture, values, religion, origin, or based on false assumptions should be avoided.

'How to say' is the speaker's demeanour. His dress and posture all affect the impact of the message. The other relevant elements are articulation, voice modulation, rate of speech, voice quality, pace, tone, volume, and emotions. The medium pitch is the most effective for conveying firmness, confidence, and authority. A high pitch is useful for reaching out to someone at a distance or talking to someone in a crowded room full of noise.

Delivering the message with care and empathy is also important, considering the receiver's background, culture, and origin. This helps ensure the receiver understands the message as intended.

Effective verbal communication helps build strong relationships—in all spheres of life. People always remember a person who speaks effectively, confidently, and charismatically.

People good at verbal communication can confidently, and easily ask questions or provide information. They know how to represent their words so that people can easily listen and understand.

Written Communication

- Written messages—as crucial as oral ones—are transmitted to receivers through letters, memos, reports, emails, and messages (including WhatsApp, Instagram, LinkedIn, and Facebook).
- Although written messages take more time to compose than verbal ones, they have distinct advantages of accuracy, precision, longevity, and legal acceptance.

- Care must be taken so the receiver can easily decipher the messages' scripts, alphabets, acronyms, logos, and graphics.

Visual Communication

Visual communication draws on a range of elements to convey ideas, attitudes, and values through visual media. Graphic designs, charts, pictures, cartoons, drawings, signs, illustrations, and animations can encapsulate complex concepts—truly illustrating that 'a picture is worth a thousand words.' They are effective in evoking high emotions and feelings or inspiring change. An eye-catching message, whether through text, graphics, or videos, informs, educates, motivates, and engages viewers.

Visual communication conveys the main points more efficiently and interestingly. The viewer is easily able to visualise its relevance to their life. Engaging the audience through a powerful story makes an impact, enhancing the recall value of the complex message.

Coming back to verbal communication, here are some of the skills required for effective verbal communication:

A. *Reinforcement*: Use of encouraging words along with non-verbal gestures such as head nods, a warm facial expression and direct eye contact to show warmth, openness, and interest in what others say. Reduce shyness or nervousness, allay fears, and encourage participation. Finally, build rapport and strengthen relationships.
B. *Questioning*: An essential element in obtaining full information and clarification and seeking explicit support from others. It is valuable for starting conversations, drawing someone into a conversation, or showing interest.

The questions could be closed (limiting the scope of the response) to seek only a one or two-word answer (simply 'yes' or 'no'). *'Did you travel by car today?' 'Did you see the football game yesterday?'* The questioner remains in control—to help focus the discussion and obtain clear, concise answers.

Alternatively, open questions are preferable for further probing, elaboration, and broadening the scope for response. *'What was the traffic like this morning?' 'What would you like to gain from this discussion?'* Open questions will take longer to answer, but they give better scope for self-expression and encourage involvement in the conversation.

Questioning could also be used to obtain a desirable outcome: *'Could I pray when I smoke?'* will get you permission in preference to *'Could I smoke when I pray?'*

C. *Reflecting and Clarifying*: Paraphrasing a message helps convey that it has been received and ensures you understand its essence. This allows the speaker to clarify or elaborate if they wish. By actively reflecting on the message, you show respect for the speaker and their perspective, making this a highly valuable skill in counselling.

D. *Summarising and Closing*: Summarising allows both parties to review the issues discussed and reach a final agreement. It lays down, in clear terms, the way forward. Both verbal and non-verbal signals are used to end a conversation. *'Well, I must be going', 'Thank you so much; that is helpful'.* However, non-verbal cues like avoiding eye contact, standing up, refusing to offer a handshake, turning away, looking at a watch, or closing the notepad would convey a disagreement.

4

Verbal Communication Skills Effective Speaking

Verbal communication is one of the most important mediums for establishing trust and building lasting relationships. It allows you to interact, engage, and collaborate to achieve positive outcomes. It is also one of the fastest and most time-efficient modes of communication.

It helps in:

- Speedy and efficient decision-making to save time and money.
- Avoiding confusion and ambiguity.
- Increasing organisational efficiency and productivity.
- Building strong interpersonal relationships and collaboration.
- Making you become more confident and a well-rounded professional.

Of the two basic Verbal Skills to communicate effectively, namely *Effective Speaking and Active Listening*, we will examine the first one now and Active Listening in the next chapter.

Effective Speaking

The speaker is responsible and accountable for getting their message across to the listener. The speaker must ensure that their message reaches the listener and that the content received by the listener is the same as the speaker intended. To achieve this, the speaker must:

1. Ensure they have the listener's full attention. To this end, the speaker should be careful that:
   - The line of vision between the two is clear in a physical meeting. The listener is not busy with any other activity and is mentally available.
   - In all other cases, the speaker must get verbal confirmation that the listener is available.
2. Ensure their physical appearance is not disturbing. Their looks, behaviour, and manners should be pleasant. A warm, engaging smile, a firm handshake, and a salutation will do the trick.
3. To engage with the listener, they should:
   - Organise their thoughts and speak concisely, with clarity, friendliness, awareness, positivity, and dignity.
   - Be soft-spoken and avoid hurting people. People who talk politely and with a smile are readily accepted, making the interaction enjoyable.
   - Choose the right tone of voice (positive, confident—no sarcasm), pitch, curiosity, and responsiveness. Also, modulate the tone to suit the words and feelings.
   - Choose their words and non-verbal gestures considering the listener's sensitivities, feelings, and cultural factors,

which influence the content of messages. Use simple language if a foreign accent is heard.

- Note that the 'what' and 'how' you speak to a close colleague in a discussion will differ considerably from how you present the topic in a large conference.

4. As the conversation progresses, the speaker should note:
   - The verbal responses made by the listener. These will confirm that the message's contents have reached them as intended.
   - The non-verbal cues emanate from the listener. Facial expressions reiterate interest, commitment, mental state, and focus.
   - Incorrect or partial receipt of the message will result in an incorrect outcome. Enquire directly if there is any doubt.
5. Finally, the two sides should be able to arrive at a decision, which is the purpose of the conversation. Both sides should verbalise the decision in their own words to eliminate confusion. Later, it should be put down in writing and exchanged.

5

Verbal Communication Skills Active Listening

Communication is vital to our existence, and the interpersonal skill of Active Listening is crucial for effective communication. Communication is a two-way street, and you will not get far if you do not listen attentively. Avoid interrupting or responding until you have heard the full message and had time to process it. Impatience and poor listening are at the root of most conflicts, arguments, fights, and even wars.

The Process

The process of listening starts with 'hearing'—the physical act of registering the sound waves in the ears. Dedicated nerves transfer the sound from the ears to the brain.

Communication includes 'non-verbal' communication received in the brain through other senses, such as our eyes or touch.

On arrival, the brain processes the information against the existing data (past experiences) to derive meaning (recognising a pattern).

The information received through the communication listened to will be the basis for a response—action, reaction, or inaction.

Pointers for Effective Active Listening

- To 'listen' to a speaker with all senses, be present—give undivided attention; put aside distracting thoughts and environmental stimuli. Stop talking—whether sitting across physically or on an electronic device (mobile, laptop or multitasking).
- Be silent—in both body and spirit—emanating positive signals and delivering energy. *Mansaa Vachaa Karmanaa* (मनसा वाचा कर्मणा—thoughts, words, and deed). Stay calm, control your emotions, and remain composed. Silence and focus provide you the emotional energy needed to truly understand the other person's message, saving you both time and effort. Without this, you will remain in mere 'hearing' mode, rather than truly listening.
- Maintain eye contact—a natural, gentle gaze—to make the speaker comfortable and assure them you are listening to their words, emotions, and feelings. You sincerely wish to help them solve their problem, whether you agree with it or not. If both listener and speaker look into each other's eyes, all communication gaps or challenges are addressed.
- Ensure you are a part of and enjoy the interaction through your demeanour—body, eyes, and space—to listen to non-verbal cues.
- Listen with an open mind, empathy, and humility to understand the speaker's intent. Everyone has a perspective, so respect the views and thoughts of others. Listen with

patience, maintaining a smiling demeanour. Focus on the speaker rather than planning your response or dwelling on the questions you have in mind. Defer judgement seek first to understand, then to be understood.

- Allow the speaker to vent their emotions. Support them positively with a smile, nods, and exclamations with gestures like—hmm, yes, next, I understand, I see, I agree.
- Pay attention to the primary points in the speaker's message. Grasp the gist of what they are trying to communicate and the specific words used. Interrupting them will miss their meaning and is also considered rude. Next, summarise the speaker's message to convey your understanding and assure them you understand the issue. Discussing comparable situations and verbalising empathy will connect you better.
- Seek clarifications and ask pointed questions to complete the picture and cover the gaps. Providing positive feedback—communication is a two-way street—completes the loop to obtain a favourable outcome. Keep repeating the give-and-take process or negotiations until both sides reach a consensus—to agree or disagree, fully or partially.
- Remember, two people with different natures and attitudes are involved. They also are operating from different levels, emotions, and perspectives. Patience, respect, and assertive responses on either side will go a long way towards a positive outcome.
- After you have a clear picture of the issues involved, reflect on them before responding; do not rush. Your response should be honest and transparent. Include the reasons for your reply, advice, or comments. Notably, instead of a blunt NO, offer them choices—with reasons—to neutralise the sting.
- Taking notes while listening will be a great help.

A listening event may not take place or could get compromised on several counts:

- Overpowering noise in the environment, a sound that is too soft, or ears that are not in receiving condition may impair hearing.
- Your mind is not in a 'Listening' mode: The sound has reached the brain, but it is not being registered effectively, as you are distracted. This distraction could be due to your judgement about the speaker or the subject being discussed, or you may have missed important non-verbal cues. While you have 'heard' the words, you missed the essence of the message.
- Listening will not occur if you are not empathetic to the speaker or are distracted by the delivery method or non-verbal cues displayed by the speaker—including voice tone and body signals.
- The distractions mostly occur when you are busy framing your response rather than listening to the entire message.
- We jump in with our immediate retort to show dominance or indicate, 'I know'. There is a physical reason for this: Thoughts travel faster than speech. Your brain races ahead with the reply even though the speaker has not yet finished the message.
- Looking at your watch or phone regularly, sighing audibly, doodling, or tapping a pen conveys your disinterest and disrespect, making the speaker feel uncomfortable and frustrated.

Benefits of Active Listening

Active listening improves focus and concentration. You build rapport with the speaker, convey your care, and turn them into your ardent fan. You are less likely to make mistakes when dealing with the issue, and your replies will be received well.

Master this art—it goes beyond skill—and you will see your reputation as a great conversationalist flourish. All you need to do is listen attentively, interjecting with searching questions. You may not contribute to the conversation, but they will still treat you respectfully.

It creates an environment where ideas, feedback, and information flow freely and accurately to build cohesive teams in the workplace, at home, or on the road. You also manage conflicts and address misunderstandings better.

Become an active listener with your team—the first point of contact with the clients—the results will amaze you! You will win the hearts and loyalty of your team members and help them become active listeners with the clients. In effect, you are extending your circle of influence, leading to a positive outcome.

Developing this soft skill will help you build and maintain connections, open collaboration opportunities, solve problems, and improve expectations. When team members or clients feel they can speak openly with you—without interruptions, judgement, or unwelcome interjections—they are more likely to trust and confide in you. This, in turn, allows you to learn new insights and grow your knowledge base.

Whether you are seeking a new job opportunity, striving to earn a promotion, or working to improve your current role, improving this skill will help you succeed. It adds value to your critical thinking and conflict resolution skills.

In sum, 'ACTIVE LISTENING' means being PRESENT with the speaker, listening to the entire message, comprehending the information, and responding thoughtfully. 'I appreciate your point of view, whether I agree with it or not.' Followed in letter and spirit, it would lead to creativity and positive outcomes. Active Listening takes time and practice to develop. The more you apply this skill, the more natural it will become.

6

Non-Verbal Communication

In face-to-face interactions, non-verbal communications are signals or wordless messages conveyed through movements, gestures, actions, facial expressions, and attitudes. Most of the time, we use them unknowingly. They convey our feelings, thoughts, and perceptions about our character, impact, and credibility. This study of body language is known as Kinesics.

Non-verbal cues can make up as much as 67 per cent of communication, with over half of these signals occurring within the first six seconds of being seen. Therefore, spoken words convey only a portion of our message: 'Your actions speak louder than words.'

In the wild, animals mimic their surroundings for protection. By taking on the colour and texture of their environment, they can remain hidden and safe from predators. Human beings may also mimic for protection, taking on the mannerisms and opinions of those around us to fit in with social conformity.

Such events are mostly involuntary—we may not even realise that our colour has changed to blend in with the environment. Our non-verbal clues may sometimes become giveaways, contradicting what we express verbally. As we age, we learn to manage our emotions, concealing our inner thoughts. We learn to focus more on beautiful packaging than the gift. Dressing impeccably and changing dresses to suit the occasion is a part of this phenomenon.

That is why we are advised not to 'judge a book by its cover' or not to judge people by their appearance.

As smart listeners and intelligent conversationalists, we must master the art of observing the speakers and their body language—be sensitive to unspoken messages. This will require focus and awareness of the surroundings without embarrassing the speaker. The key is to focus on the eyes—the most reliable window into a person's mind. Listen to the other person patiently, occasionally nodding your head in affirmation.

As a speaker, you must be highly conscious—how is your body behaving, and what signals is it conveying to the listener? Speak at a moderate rate, with clarity to synchronise with your body signals.

The following aspects of non-verbal communication help create positive and lasting impressions:

- Hygiene, grooming, and smart, clean, and ironed dresses add value to appearance.
- A firm body stance with a relaxed posture shows liveliness and energy, making people more comfortable.
- A relaxed face conveys confidence and high integrity.
- A firm, relaxed handshake with a smile and direct eye contact conveys an open-arms attitude and welcome. Limp or bone-crusher handshakes are detrimental.
- A warm, open smile makes people feel relaxed and accepted. It conveys self-esteem, confidence, and well-being, making the environment lively, cool, and kicking.

'When you smile, people around you will smile too.' Tele-callers are always advised to 'Smile on the telephone so the listener can hear your smile.' Lack of eye contact raises distrust and suspicion.

- Warm, kind-hearted eye contact establishes direct communication, but prolonged gaze or 'staring' makes the other person uncomfortable, so take breaks.
- Maintain a healthy physical distance to respect the sanctity of the 'body bubble'. The distance varies and is determined by the degree of relationship, emotional status, and cultural and social norms.

Some Examples of Gestures & Postures

Body Behaviour	Indicates	Circumstances
A relaxed body with a smile.	Happiness and success.	Recognise the importance of an event.
A slumped body with a frown.	Sadness and failure.	Create dejection.
Leaning forward.	Enhanced concentration.	Add emphasis (in negotiations, sales).
Leaning back.	Relaxed, absorbing information.	Complex and lengthy meetings.
Clasping both hands behind the neck.	Reducing tension.	Non-threatening situations.
Glasses removed and put down.	Digesting the information.	Complex situations.
Continued straight gaze.	Failing attention.	Listening to nonsense.
Tilting head.	Listening hard.	Unending discussions.
Narrowing eyes.	Dislike.	Short on patience.

7

Open vs Closed Communication

Open and closed communication are tools for managers and leaders to foster collaboration in the workplace. In open communication, all members participate and build the team. In the other case, one communicator relays information to a group.

Open Communication

Open communication is when team members are encouraged to share their opinions, thoughts, and beliefs without fear of criticism or ridicule. The members talk to one another, share and debate ideas, ask questions, suggest improvements, and address concerns. The managers and the leaders facilitate conversations. Finally, the team arrives at a joint decision.

Closed Communication

Closed communication in the workplace is when an active communicator speaks to relay information. The information being conveyed might be their own or something passed on from others. They are instructing others to follow it.

Comparative features and benefits of the Open and Closed communications are:

Narrative	Open Communication	Closed Communication
Definition	Encourages discussions among multiple people at a workplace.	Everyone follows one person, and discussion is discouraged.
Medium	Face-to-face, phone calls, instant messaging, or videos.	Oral communication or written documents, emails.
Quality	Improved quality of decisions.	Best for uniform outcomes.
Effectiveness	Easily acceptable as it is a decision of the entire team.	Easy to implement.
Efficiency	Time-consuming, as everyone contributes to the decision-making.	Quicker action but the quality may be jeopardised.
Ease of Replication	More challenging to replicate because the outcome is discussion-dependent.	Easier to replicate as the same message is delivered to multiple groups or locations.
Questioning	What? Where? Why? Who? When? How?	Not allowed.

Narrative	Open Communication	Closed Communication
Benefits	Builds trust and loyalty in the team; improves confidence; establishes ownership of the decision; and achieves greater productivity.	Gets you faster and uniform results, at multiple locations. However, it does not work in the long run.

Open communication is undoubtedly a better bet for an organisation that aims to grow exponentially in a healthy environment. It improves engagement, promotes inclusion, supports employee happiness, reduces cultural disparity, clarifies expectations, and builds trust and strong relationships.

It also reduces errors, enhances quality and productivity, fosters creativity and innovation, and improves outcomes. The entire team learns the decision-making process, thereby developing future leaders. It helps enhance self-confidence, aligns with the team's goals, and creates loyalty and a commitment to the organisation's vision. The downside is that it is a time-consuming process.

Closed communication is the best bet where quick decision-making and timely action are paramount, and uniformity is a desired outcome. Otherwise, it is the antithesis of a healthy environment in an organisation.

The Individual

8

Communication Styles

Style is a powerful tool for managing the impact of communication in a continuum and achieving the desired outcomes. Different styles help build attitudes and behaviours to control your environment—at the workplace (your teams) and in your personal space to build great relationships—to operate at a subtle level and on a long-term basis.

We communicate with others using three distinct styles. These styles reflect the degree of respect:

i. An *Aggressive style* involves demanding that others give to you.
ii. A *Passive style* means you are yielding to others' demands.
iii. An *Assertive style* allows you to express your intentions and objectives clearly and confidently.

They reflect your situation (time and place), station (weaker or powerful), or relationship (unknown, close, or distant).

1. *Aggressive*: An aggressive communication style is used when you value your rights—perceived or in real terms—higher than those of others. You tell people, 'This is what I want, and what you want is unimportant.' 'I do not care what you feel about it—my way or highway.' 'I'm right, and you are wrong.' 'I will get my way no matter what. It is all your fault.'

   You tend to dominate others, using put-downs and violating their rights. The other side may ultimately feel dominated or humiliated by your communication, and you may attract retaliatory action later.

   Such communications have Win-Lose consequences.
2. *Passive*: In this style, you surrender your rights in favour of others. You are conveying:
   - You tend to say 'Yes' when you want to say 'No'. You want to avoid conflict as you have serious doubts about handling the situation.
   - You are operating from a weaker position and are surrendering.
   - You are apologetic and scared to express your feelings and thoughts honestly.
   - For reasons—known or unknown—you wish to please others. 'It really does not matter much'; 'I just want to keep the peace.'
   - You feel contradiction will lead to demeaned and humiliated situations, and you feel keeping the peace is a better option.

Your stand would generally lead to Lose-Win consequences.

3. *Assertive*: A style practised by winners.
   - Being assertive involves conveying your stand, request, or need firmly in simple, clear, honest, and straightforward terms.

- You express yourself without humiliating, dominating, or insulting others. 'I understand I have choices, and I will consider my options.'
- Implicitly or explicitly, you are conveying that you respect both your rights and the rights of others.
- It would help immensely if you explained the reasons for your stand to the other side upfront and in detail. The urgency and importance of the circumstances or reasons would easily persuade the other side to accept your stand.
- Sharing the reasons would also create an environment for exploring common grounds to help identify a Win-Win solution in which neither side should feel let down. Both will feel satisfied and valued. Listen with empathy, look at things from both perspectives and see the situation as an opportunity to devise alternatives.
- Changing the style of questioning to elicit positive responses will help: 'Can I smoke when I pray?' Or 'Can I pray while I smoke?' Offer choices/options to get the desired response, a skill that requires practice.
- The assertive style is highly recommended to build healthy relationships and get desired outcomes. It helps you to be in command of a situation or an event to achieve your long-term goals.
- In principle, assertive communication is the best style to adopt and practice, particularly in personal relationships.
- This style may not be the best choice in dealing with obstinate people who may pressure you to do something you would rather avoid. Or in negotiations or where it damages your relationship on a long-term basis.

The following examples will make it easy to understand the nuances of the three styles:

Situation	Response	Style Used in the Response	Suggested Assertive Response
A group of colleagues are fixing their next get-together. You are keen to join in, but the date accepted by everyone else is impossible for you.	'Well, all right, as it seems to suit everyone else.'	Passive	I would like to be part of it. Would Wednesday suit everybody?
A colleague interrupts you when you are busy on an important phone call.	'I would like to finish this call, then I will be happy to have a word with you.'	Assertive	'I would like to finish this call, then I will be happy to have a word with you.'
Your boss praises the way you handled an awkward customer.	'It was nothing, really. Sunita did all the hard work, and I only came in at the end.'	Passive	Thanks. It is great teamwork. I would like to add that Sunita put in a lot of hard work. (We generally cannot handle praise.)

Situation	Response	Style Used in the Response	Suggested Assertive Response
Your subordinate has just returned to the office after a four-day absence, despite having been approved leave only for two days.	'You are always doing this! That is the last time you will be allowed on this flimsy excuse.'	Aggressive	This needs to be discussed—how it could be avoided in future. (I would like to know the real reason why you have spent two extra days on leave.)
Your boss has sent a memo saying, all staff must smile at customers in future. You are unhappy with this.	'I am not happy with this ruling. I feel it should be left to me to judge each situation on its merit. Can I discuss this with you please?'	Assertive	'I am not happy with this ruling. I feel it should be left to me to judge each situation on its merit. Can I discuss this with you please?'
A customer demands a seat on an aircraft in a non-smoking area even though you have explained that they are already allocated.	'You should have booked in earlier if you wanted to get a non-smoking seat.'	Aggressive	We have given priority to those who booked in advance. Please wait, I will find out if a passenger would agree to a change.

Situation	Response	Style Used in the Response	Suggested Assertive Response
You want to buy a mobile and the salesman is pushing hard to buy another model, which is more expensive than you intended. You had thought of looking at several models before deciding.	'Well, it is what I was looking for. I suppose they are all the much the same and there is not much point in shopping around.'	Passive	I intend to see other models as well before I decide. Could you help? (I am looking for a more affordable model within my budget.)
Your partner asks you sarcastically what went wrong with the dinner preparations (It was not yet ready).	'If you expect me to be at your beck and call, you better think again. Try getting your own dinner.'	Aggressive	I am running late, and I would like you to help me by laying the table.
A neighbour agreed to babysit for you and then failed to turn up. You telephone and say.	'Nandita, I understood you were going to babysit for us tonight. Has something happened?'	Assertive	'Nandita, I understood you were going to babysit for us tonight. Has something happened?'

Situation	Response	Style Used in the Response	Suggested Assertive Response
A friend asks you for a lift. It is inconvenient for you as you are late already, and the drive will take you out of your way.	'I am already late, so I cannot take you all the way. If it helps, I will drop you off at the bus stop.'	Assertive	'I am already late, so I cannot take you all the way. If it helps, I will drop you off at the bus stop.'

Style Strategy

In his treatise Arthashastra, Chanakya (Kautilya), mentor of great King Chandragupta Maurya (324 BCE to 293 BCE), recommends using different approaches for achieving an outcome:

> साम,
> *Saam* (persuade, advise, address disagreements)
> दाम,
> *Daam* (buyout, bribe, reward, recognise)
> दंड,
> *Dand* (threaten, punish)
> भेद,
> *Bhed* (secret, divide and rule, blackmail)

He recommends using any or all these styles, but always with a positive intent for the common good, aiming to improve a situation rather than worsen it. He identified these styles as essential for providing effective and benevolent governance.

The three communication styles, in principle, reflect a modern interpretation of Chanakya's approach. Students and practitioners of commerce, finance, politics, and diplomacy have successfully used these styles in negotiations from time immemorial. These are also effective for building great teams.

None of the styles is better than the other; they are situation-dependent. Experienced negotiators move from one to another fluidly, subtly, and not in a particular order. The trick is to practice the styles over an extended period with positivity, patience, empathy, and persistence—understanding the nuances, assessing strengths and weaknesses, keeping emotions in check, and avoiding an intent to hurt others.

In the context of verbal and non-verbal signals, the cues used in communication styles are:

Aggressive	Passive	Assertive
Non-Verbal Signals		
Usually, in a shouty, loud, no-choice voice.	Whiny, yes-man voice; my rights do not exist.	Calm, relaxed, even voice; exuding confidence.
Dominating tone.	Meek tone.	Firm tone.
Dominating, intimidating posture; red face; folded arms; pointing finger.	Clenched, wringing hands; shuffling feet; weak posture.	Relaxed posture (comfortable with oneself).
Bulging, aggressive eyes.	Avoiding eye-to-eye contact.	Direct eye-to-eye contact.
Creating a vicious environment.	Merging in the background.	Firm and relaxed stance.
Bossy approach.	Avoids speaking up.	Honest approach.
Others' rights do not exist.	Gets stepped on.	Respects others' rights.

Aggressive	Passive	Assertive
Reactive communicator.	Accommodative communicator.	Effective communicator.
My way or highway.	Avoids conflict.	Aware of one's choices.
Is not prepared to listen to the other side.	Allows people to take advantage.	A clear statement of one's expectations and choices.
Verbal (Key Words and Expressions)		
You would better…	Maybe…	I…
If you do not…	I guess…	I think…
Watch out…	I wonder…	I feel…
Come on…	Would you mind very much if…	I wish…
This is what I want you to do…	Maybe...	Let us see how we can do it together…
Useless.	Excuse me, please.	How can we resolve this?
Stupid.	Whatever you say.	What do you think?
You…	You are right.	What do you see?
I want this to be done this way.	We will do it.	I hope you do not mind.

9

Communication in Leaders' Influencing Styles

Leadership is about inspiring your team to work on a goal that becomes the achievement of the entire team.

The leaders have their roles clearly defined at several levels. They:

- Take ownership of a vision for their organisation, institution, society, or nation and identify specific goals for implementing this vision.
- Identify the team to help them achieve the goal.
- Influence the team and its members to adopt the goals as a shared objective, turning the leader's goal into 'their goal.'
- Guide the team and create the roadmap to achieve the goal.
- Work alongside the team to set the organisation on an exponential growth path.

Influencing is *the capacity to* impact a team's ideas, opinions, and actions. *Leaders,* motivators, influencers, and advisors use this valuable tool to build strong team relationships in a collaborative environment to implement their vision. *Influencing is a state of mind, not by designation, and is a decisive step.*

While influencing has always been a valuable leadership skill, it has become essential in today's fast-paced and stressful work environment. Success depends on your ability to influence not only your direct reports but also those connected indirectly, including the clients.

Several influencing styles are available to leaders, including:

> Accommodative, Affiliative, Assertive, Autocratic, Bridging, Cautious, Charismatic, Coaching, Collaborative, Commanding, Democratic, Delegative, Dominating, Driving, Empowering, Educating, Goal Presentation, Inspiring, Institutionalising, Negotiating, Participative, Pushing, Problem-Solving, Rationalising, Reflective, Supportive, and Visionary.

Of these, the following have found more favour with successful leaders:

1. *AUTOCRATIC STYLE*:

Highly opinionated, autocratic leaders make decisions without reference to anyone else. They are obsessed with doing things more, faster, better, and with perfection. They set high standards and have little patience with poor performers.

This style gets you the best results in times of crisis—where hard decisions must be made quickly and decisively. Later, perhaps, the team can go into action-result relationships.

This will add to the experience and build historical data for similar situations.

The downsides of this style are that it alienates the team, demotivates, and makes them overly reliant on the leader. At some point, the team may revolt against you. Like a horse that moves forward when whipped, it will only do so again at the cost of needing another whip to make it move.

2. *VISIONARY STYLE*:

Self-confident, self-aware, and empathetic leaders use a visionary style. They strongly believe in and take responsibility for their vision. They inspire the team by bringing meaning and positive direction by explaining, exploring, describing, and selling the vision. They consult, solicit suggestions—with commitment, integrity, and honesty—and then delegate for delivery.

They ensure their vision is value-driven and aligned with the organisational values that help you distinguish between good and evil, important and unimportant, deep and superficial, and moral and immoral.

This style would be ineffective from a short-term perspective when it fails to consider the natural talents and experience of the knowledgeable team members. The leader will succeed only if they regularly refresh the team's vision.

3. DEMOCRATIC STYLE:

A democratic leader picks a committed and competent team that can achieve their goals independently through engagement and participation in a long-term perspective. This style builds an effective team operating with a Win-Win approach, where everyone takes ownership of the goals and ideas in a transparent and fair environment.

Highly involving, motivating and persuasive, it encourages decision-making from different perspectives through consensus. Consultation improves the sharing of ideas and experiences within the business.

The Democratic Style is least effective in a crisis where immediate response is required. Or where the individuals are incompetent or need close supervision. It also will not give results when complete information is not shared, or everyone involved is not heard.

4. *EMPOWERMENT STYLE:*

The leader gives authority and responsibility to make decisions by creating a culture of empowerment.

The Culture of Inclusion (everybody must feel included)—to create owners.

The Culture of Creating Confidence (avoiding 'I know you will fail')—give input, do not investigate the past.

The Culture of Results (fight on the target, but once it is decided, it must be achieved)—birds fly together.

The Culture of Learning (mistakes to be viewed in an appropriate light, learn from them) provides a learning platform.

The Culture of Celebration (even for small victories and even in a small way—nukkad chai, an ice cream—no need to call a meeting). Go to the source and celebrate with whoever is available.

Culture of Managing Change—ultimately, change is inevitable and defines the game.

5. NEGOTIATING STYLE:

People with this style seek a better outcome using compromises (concessions, trade-offs) to seek common ground. They are strong collaborators, seeking to accommodate different interests and make room for all voices to be heard. They use personal relationships and rely on reciprocity to create consensus and harmony.

They are active listeners, advisers, emotional supporters, counsellors, and providers of constructive feedback. Selfless in nature, they make everyone feel valued, offer social support, and reward achievements. They avoid making hasty decisions and often find intelligent, workable solutions to problems.

The downside is that if they compromise with their principles, the opportunists will outmanoeuvre them. Also, the style only works in the short run as the collaborators with diverse interests become impatient with each other.

Influencing is an inherent part of our life journey in life. People naturally affect and are affected by those they encounter—be it colleagues, friends, or family. While influential people may appear to have a natural talent, the ability to motivate and influence others is a skill that can be learned. However, it requires effort in honing your communication skills.

Communication skills cannot be learned from textbooks; they evolve after you leave school. Most top leaders developed their styles by watching others and gathering experiences—learning through mistakes—Mahatma Gandhi, Narasimha Rao, Narayana Murthy, Azim Premji, Warren Buffet, and Bill Gates are some influential people who honed and used their communication skills to the fullest.

The first step toward improving your communication skills and using them wisely is identifying your inclinations when interacting with others and gaining insight into the styles used by others and the results they get. This practice will help you recognise with whom and when your approach is working brilliantly and when it is not working. With experience, you will improve your outcomes.

To become an effective influencer, the following pointers may be helpful:

- All styles are adequate; there is no good or bad style. All leaders have a natural influencing style and skilfully switch styles depending on the situation.
- Mastering the influencing styles is like learning a new language. It takes practice, patience, and persistence. Keep an open mind with empathy. You do not know all the problems or solutions. Be aware of your body language. Just like your words, your body language is sending the messages.
- Ask questions and listen carefully. Notice the tone, body language, and how people structure their ideas. What are their concerns? When are they most animated? When are they excited? When people say or do something, it reveals what motivates them. This needs to be observed.
- Be aware of the influencing style team members use in each interaction. Meet them using the communication style they are most comfortable with. Pay close attention to how your influence is received. Adapt as the interaction progresses.

10

Communication in Relationships

Life is transactional, continuous buying and selling. We like to do business or make friends with whom we are comfortable and can trust. Thus, relationships are the building blocks of success and a fulfilling future. Focus on them; you will make a positive difference in your environment and your job will become less of a toil and more enjoyable. Your colleagues and clients will become your friends. The achievement of desired results will follow automatically.

Communication is the key to building trust and relationships. It is the fundamental element that holds all relationships together. To communicate effectively to build relationships, we need to focus on the following pointers:

1. *First Impression*: Be decently dressed. Be organised and carry out research before the meeting. Be approachable and learn names correctly and quickly. Be attentive and appreciative; show admiration.

2. *Face-to-face*: You are dealing with another human being, meeting them in person to establish genuine connections and collaboration. Respect and acknowledge their presence. Be honest and sincere, and make every conversation count. Be mindful of your body language, facial expressions, and eye contact. Stay focused on the goal and be considerate of the other person's time.
3. *Content*: Use simple language without jargon.
4. *Delivery*: Be mindful of your vocal clarity, speed, pronunciation, diction, and tone of voice. Adding light humour and mild teasing will make the conversation lively.
5. *Listen*: Hear, process, and respond to what the other person is saying. Take a keen interest in them and use appropriate verbal and non-verbal door-openers. Ask questions to encourage a conversation. Being non-judgemental will help a great deal. Be patient; do not interrupt or jump to conclusions until they complete their statement.
6. *Non-Verbal Cues*: Listening with a reclined body, distracted, and blank looks will not make friends leave aside closing business.
7. *Empathy*: Empathy is our ability to experience thoughts, emotions, and experiences mutually. It is also about caring for the other person's thoughts and feelings.
8. *Positivity*: Be humble, kind, and courteous, and make others feel important to build long-term relationships. It would help you gain a competitive edge and achieve success.
9. *Enthusiasm*: Your cheerfulness, spirit, and demeanour will win many friends. Wake up daily with a clean slate and a spring in your step, eager to take in new experiences.
10. *Be Proactive*: Take charge, break big problems into bite-size chunks, keep calm, seek help, and speak clearly. Embrace acceptance; work on improving communication. If you feel a spark is missing in your relationship, consider

working on your *Credibility*, *Consistency*, and *Confidence* to enhance your likeability.

11. *Small Talk*: Plays a crucial role in building and strengthening relationships. Ask about their experiences, shared interests, and opinions to make them comfortable.
12. *Conflict*: A certain amount of friction is inevitable when working in a relationship. If conflict is not handled immediately, a minor dispute can become a serious confrontation. Shouting, sarcasm, complaining, blaming, issuing threats, and throwing insults will spiral into negativity. When we react defensively, we often interrupt and raise our voices—disturbing the listening part.
13. *Forgive*: By forgiving, you will win your friends forever. You will also be at peace with yourself.
14. *Reflection*: Before you let the words escape, think carefully. Slow down to weigh the impact of what you are going to say.
15. *Repetition*: When paraphrasing something differently from how it was delivered, you clarify your understanding and stimulate further discussion. You also give confidence to the other person you are paying attention to.
16. *Restriction*: To maintain positivity, avoid negative words like always, never, should, maybe, but you must, and cannot.
17. *Written Messages*: Email, instant messages, chat rooms, social media, etc., have thrown enormous challenges. Our written language should be simple, courteous, straightforward, and conversational. Clear, concise, accurate language gives an impression of efficiency and fills the reader with confidence.

11

Communication in Self-Talk

One of the least discussed aspects of communication is self-talk or intrapersonal skills. Self-talk is the voice inside your head, your imagination, visualisation, and even recalling past events. These internal abilities and behaviours regulate the self: managing emotions, coping with challenges, and exploring new information.

This internal conversation occurs continuously while you are busy with daily activities, an ongoing process that rarely stops. It is significant because you are the only person constantly communicating with yourself, 24/7.

Research has shown that positive self-talk improves your body's response. It helps you manage your emotional intelligence with energy, self-confidence, self-discipline, focus, resilience, and persistence.

Being open to new ideas enhances your execution skills: planning, problem-solving, conflict resolution, evaluation, judgement, adaptability to change, and more. Build solid relationships, trust, and rapport with your team and achieve your goals.

Conversely, if you believe you cannot do something, your brain will tell your body to shut down. Your self-talk can help you respond constructively if you are angry or frustrated.

Techniques to Improve Self-talk:

1. *Make time for Self-reflection*: Reflect on your actions, beliefs, priorities, and choices. Consider what is important in your life, such as personal values and loved ones. What brings joy and fulfilment?
2. *Active Listening to Self*: Listen to your feelings and thoughts to develop self-awareness and understanding. Ask yourself questions and reflect on the responses.
3. *Be Kind and Compassionate*: Love yourself, even during setbacks. Cultivate a positive self-image to diminish negativity.
4. *Develop a Routine*: Practising mindfulness, journaling, yoga, and meditation can greatly help improve your relationship with yourself.
5. *Mindfulness*: Mindfulness is about being present and conscious, free from judgement or distractions. Spending time in a quiet space—without mobiles, social media, or emails—can be helpful.
6. *Journaling*: Writing down your thoughts and experiences helps you identify patterns in your thinking and develop greater self-awareness.
7. *Yoga and Meditation*: Helping you maintain a healthy body, manage stress and anxiety, and develop stability.
8. *Seek Support*: Talk to a friend or family member or seek professional help to gain new insights and perspectives into your thought process.

9. *Visualisation*: Involves creating mental images of desired outcomes or situations. It helps build confidence, motivation, and a positive outlook.
10. *Goal Setting*: Set realistic but stretched goals to align them with your values and priorities to develop a sense of purpose and direction.
11. *Self-Affirmations*: Affirm your worth and capabilities to develop a more positive self-image, self-confidence and self-esteem and achieve whatever you desire.

Intrapersonal communication is an ongoing process. Feel free to try new things and see what works best for you!

Benefits of Positive Self-talk	Risks of Negative Self-talk
Better coping skills during times of hardship and stress.	Chronic stress.
Better psychological and physical well-being.	Poor mental and physical health.
Increased life span, better cardiovascular health, and reduced risk of death.	Low quality of life.
Reduced rates of depression and distress.	Low self-esteem.
Adding value, one at a time.	Perfectionism.
Responding to incidents and interactions with others.	Resistance to change.
Optimistic and supportive attitude.	Vain.
Regulated emotions.	Enhanced remorse, decreased confidence, and restricted personal achievement.

Self-Concept

Self-concept refers to how individuals view themselves, including their beliefs, values, and attitudes. Life experiences, relationships, and cultural background shape self-concept.

Self-talk gives you a healthy self-concept. A positive self-concept enhances self-esteem and confidence, while a negative self-concept can lead to self-doubt, pessimism, or guilt. If you picture yourself as pleasant and engaging, others will see you as attractive.

Cultivating a positive self-concept typically means 'tooting your own horn' but with positivity. Create an optimistic scenario, act positively, and shun negative beliefs and social comparisons.

Self-Love

Self-concept leads to self-love, which means accepting yourself as 'a great person'. Embrace who you are unconditionally, with your strengths and weaknesses.

Self-love is closely related to self-esteem, self-compassion, and your love for yourself. Understanding your value positively affects well-being, mental fitness, and relationships.

Self-talk becomes a desirable and happy practice when conjoined with Self-concept and Self-love. Together, they add enormous value to your life. Embrace challenges with enthusiasm and grow with joy!

12

Communication in Public Speaking

Public speaking is a one-to-many communication. You share your thoughts to inform, influence, decide, or close a deal with a large gathering.

A must-have communication skill for politicians, leaders, business owners, executives, and educationists to build support, trust, respect, and credibility.

Truisms in Public Speaking

Addressing a crowd—cutting across cultures—remains one of the most common fears in the universe. Most speakers develop butterflies whenever they get onto the podium. A few have natural talent; most must train hard to master this complex art. The more often you speak, the better you become—IF *you learn from your mistakes.*

The main ingredients of speech-making are thoughts and emotions, and the technique to deliver them in a structured way to make the audience buy into your views.

Complexity in public speaking arises because speech is mostly a monologue (except for the brief Question and Answer session).

To be an effective speaker, you have two tasks cut out for you:

1. Deliver your message clearly and impactfully to achieve the desired outcome.
2. Be attentive to the non-verbal feedback from your audience to assess whether your message is resonating with them. Be ready to adjust your presentation accordingly.

To achieve these goals, you must plan carefully:

1. **Preparations**
   i. Identify the purpose of the speech and the audience's expectations. Research the background material thoroughly. It is wise to focus on a specific aspect rather than attempting to cover the entire subject. This approach will increase your confidence and help establish your authority.
   ii. Compose the speech concisely and precisely, keeping the time limit and audience takeaway in mind. Include the right pitch, anecdotes, and stories to engage your listeners.
   iii. Practise, practise, and practise. Presenters who seem naturally unscripted or 'off the cuff' often rehearse for hours. Start with small improvements, work on reducing mistakes, and practise speaking aloud, whether in front of a mirror or with a team to provide feedback. Grab every opportunity to speak in business meetings and clubs such as Toastmasters.

iv. Familiarise yourself with the venue by arriving early, allowing time to relax and manage your anxiety. Check the seating arrangements and equipment, such as whiteboards, markers, lighting, projection screen, and sound system. Loosen up, do some stretches, and refresh yourself before settling in.
v. Use written affirmations to boost your confidence.

2. **Delivery**
   i. Do not look at your mobile; keep it on silent mode.
   ii. The audience is there because they believe you have an important message to share. They are eager to hear from you and want you to succeed.
   iii. A bit of nervousness, often called 'butterflies', is perfectly normal and even beneficial. It helps to boost adrenaline and keeps you energised. begin by accepting your fear—failing would not be the end of the world, and people will quickly move on and forget.
   iv. Stand tall with your feet apart, balancing your body. Even if you feel nervous, aim to appear relaxed. Breathe deeply and smile often. Speak slowly, firmly, clearly, and with positivity—confidence will naturally come across. Be authentic, speak from the heart, and ensure your talk flows smoothly and is well-informed. Use body language effectively to emphasise key points. Non-verbal cues are often more significant than verbal ones.
   v. Avoid excessive movement—it can distract the audience. Also, avoid gimmicks, shouting, excessive or jerky movements, or dancing. Do not get stuck in one place or set eyes on one side of the hall. Make use

of the available space, but move with grace. Keep your hands free—do not hold on to objects like pencils, handkerchiefs, books, bags, or even your dress. Let your hands move naturally.

vi. Maintain eye contact, as it is the key to building a rapport with the audience. Focus on one section for 8–15 seconds, then move on to another. Engage your audience with warm, smiling eye contact and positive body language.

vii. Start by outlining what you will cover in the talk and what the audience can expect to gain from it.

viii. Next, establish your credibility by briefly reviewing your achievements and explaining why you are an authority on the subject.

ix. Share personal experiences, stories, jokes, and feelings to make your talk more engaging and relatable. Find an interesting fact or unique analogy related to your topic that few people are aware of. For example: 'Did you know when you blush, the lining of your stomach also turns red?'

x. Avoid asking questions to the audience unless the answer is expected to be a clear 'Yes' or 'No' from them.

xi. Start on time and finish on time. This will not only earn the audience's respect but also demonstrate your respect for them. Long-winded speeches can come across as arrogant and self-important.

xii. Be aware of whether your message is resonating. Signs like fidgeting, listlessness, whispering, and shifting eye contact may indicate that the audience is losing interest in the subject or the speaker. This could suggest that the topic is too complex—simplify and shorten it. Adjust your delivery style as needed.

xiii. Articulation is key to boosting your confidence and making a positive impact. Avoid mumbling, singsong, rapid-fire, or thundering styles of speaking. Adjust your pitch to suit the type of audience and subject. Lower pitches are soothing to hear, show respect and convey the relevancy of the talk in their lives. Louder pitches show energy and help build rapport. Speaking naturally and conversationally brings out the best in you and makes the audience feel personally addressed. In a confined space, use a strong voice and body language. Use an even tone and logical arguments to persuade your audience to see your point of view. Avoid the hard sell—focus on improving their professional or personal lives.

xiv. Use pauses to give both you and your audience time to reflect and absorb information. Also, pause before making an important point.

xv. If your speaking time is cut short because the previous speaker could not finish in time, do not be upset. Take it as a challenge and shorten your speech, focusing on the most crucial parts of your presentation.

xvi. Listen to the questions attentively, maintaining eye contact with the questioner. Paraphrase to confirm you have understood the question, giving yourself the time to articulate the correct answer. Avoid reacting sharply. Even if the question seems trivial, do not display any disdain, especially if the audience finds it amusing. Your response should aim to put the questioner at ease.

xvii. If you do not know the answer to a question, do not be embarrassed to admit it. Of course, you can outsmart them by saying, 'I never thought of it this way;' 'Let us all try and find the answer'; or 'What do you think the answer could be?'

xviii. If you make a mistake, do not panic. Acknowledge it, take it in your stride and continue speaking confidently. Recovering from mistakes makes you appear more human.

xix. When someone hits your hot button, take a deep breath before responding *calmly and knowledgeably. Getting angry is a big* NO. But, if the person continues to distract or engages in side conversations, politely address them by asking how you can help or whether they have a question.

xx. Conclude your talk concisely and confidently. Avoid giving false endings. Remember, a good ending only happens once.

3. **Speaker's Barriers**

   It is best to minimise the following:
   - Loud dress.
   - Leaning on a podium for the entire presentation.
   - Wringing your hands (because of nervousness).
   - Constantly gesturing with a pen and or pencil.
   - Shuffling your papers or clicking a pen.
   - Keeping your hands in your pockets.
   - Nervous pacing or not moving at all.
   - Keeping your arms crossed.
   - Inappropriate laughter.
   - Looking only at one side of the audience.

- Inappropriate medium or language such as jargon, acronyms, or technical language.
- Conveying too much or too little.
- Using an aggressive or submissive style in speaking.
- Message vague in sender's mind.
- Relying on false assumptions.
- Attributing blame, imposing guilt, or being moralistic.
- Threatening or attacking the audience's self-esteem.

4. **Review**

    i. Keep detailed notes for future use. After every speech, review your performance—what went right and what can be changed to enhance your impact.

    ii. Use high energy and empathy to overcome the communication challenges of a large audience with different experiences and viewpoints.

    iii. Avoid distrust and being judgemental to deal with differences such as gender, educational level, emotions, beliefs, cultures, and values.

    iv. Your knowledge of the subject will address your fear of public speaking.

13

Communication in Put-Downs

Put-downs are aggressive remarks intended to humiliate someone in front of others.

- Jibes, ridicules, blame, and snubs are used to humiliate, embarrass, demean, degrade, insult, or criticise contemptuously.
- Words like dumb, stupid, lazy, or expressions like 'Why didn't you…?' 'You should have…' 'You ought to…' 'You must never…' 'If you had only…' 'Don't you understand that…' 'That makes no sense at all'. 'What do you know, you're just a child?'

Such remarks harm effective communication and can damage the individual's self-esteem by making them feel rejected, unloved, and inadequate. People are put on the defensive: they get angry and want to fight back or resign to their fate. Nobody likes to be judged.

As a speaker, you must be sensitive to your messages. Do you communicate with criticism and judgement? Or with appreciation and support? Also, whether your verbal and non-verbal communications contradict each other. 'I'm interested' would be confusing if my face looked frowning and sad.

Responding assertively to put-downs is crucial for building effective, efficient, self-confident, and self-driven teams, as well as for strengthening relationships with others.

Examples:

Put Downs	Implying	Nature	Assertive
'Haven't you finished the report yet?'	'You are useless.'	Nagging	'No, when did you want it done?'
'I know I shouldn't really be nosy but...'	'I can easily get around you—you'll tell me anything.'	Prying	'Well, I won't tell you if I don't want to...'
'We should cooperate and then there would be less tension.'	'I'm ok—you should fall in line with me. It's your fault.'	Lecturing	'How could we cooperate?'
'Are you busy the day after?'	'Ha! Ha! I'll get you to agree to do what I want.'	Putting on a spot	'What did you have in mind?'

Put Downs	Implying	Nature	Assertive
'Are you sure this assignment is the right one for you?'	'You are not capable of choosing a job for yourself.'	Questioning choice	'It feels OK for me at the moment…'
'If I were you…'	'I know better than you…'	Unwanted advice	'But you are not!'
'That's a typical woman's/man's reaction…'	'You're just a stereotype—not an individual.'	Insulting labels	'It's my reaction and it's up to me to judge my own behaviour.'
'You'll find it difficult, won't you? Because you are so shy…'	'You're a hopeless case.'	Amateur psychologist	'In what ways do you think I am too shy?'

14

Communication Barriers

Communication is a sensitive subject, vulnerable to several barriers that prevent the smooth transmission of messages. These barriers must be identified and addressed as quickly as possible, as communication is the lifeline of human interaction.

The participants must have the patience and humility to accept their existence and then show respect, compassion, and empathy to work on the barriers together and deliberately so that the goal of the conversation is achieved. For this purpose, they must look within for emotional, attitudinal, perception, and psychological issues.

The barriers can occur at any stage of the communication process—at the speaker's end, at the receiver's end, or in transmission:

The Speaker's End:

- Ignorance of or failure to understand the listener's background (unfamiliarity with the language, jargon, acronyms, slang, or technical language) and perception may obstruct the latter's understanding of the message.

- Negativity or a lack of knowledge/interest towards the message or the listener.
- Bad timing of the message.
- The message is based on false assumptions, reflects prejudice, is improper, abusive, obnoxious, moralistic, gives uncalled-for advice, or conveys rejection without assigning reasons.
- Choosing the wrong content or expression, a fast-paced delivery with few pauses, speaking too much or too little, improper articulation, indecisiveness, and failing to synchronise the message, the tone, and the gestures.
- The message attributes blame, imposes guilt, or threatens the listener's self-esteem.
- The speaker blocks the feedback from the listener to thwart the intent of the communication.

The Listeners' End:

- Lack of knowledge of the subject, semantics, or communication skills.
- Lack of interest in listening to or reading between the lines.
- Selective listening or preconceived notions, prejudices, ideas & opinions about the speaker, indulging in mind reading.
- Urge to retort, react, or interfere without listening to the entire message.
- Non-concentration, distractions due to physical or mental condition, passivity, boredom, or tiredness.
- Inability to provide proper feedback.
- Lacking the capacity to process large amounts of information or data.

In Transmission:

- Physical or environmental.
- Inappropriate selection of communication mediums or channels.
- Participants' learning, culture, values, beliefs, language, and semantic skills differ.
- The message flows through a long chain of participants.

Written Communication Barriers:

Written communications, including letters, curriculum vitae, emails, project reports, and legal briefs, are used to manage company operations, close a sale, and build business dealings and its image.

Barriers such as misspelt names, typo-filled documents, unfinished drafts, or passive-aggressive messages can distort the content of the messages, resulting in communication breakdown:

Some serious barriers could be messages forwarded to the wrong addressee, un-replied emails, casual forwarding of annoying documents, or using unwanted language or words.

Barriers Mitigation:

- 'Know *your purpose*, listen with ears of *tolerance*, see through the eyes of *compassion* and speak with *the language of love.*'
- Shift to another location or use technology in case of physical or environmental barriers (including noise, static, fog, dust, clutter, stress, and conflict).
- Direct eye contact, a smiling face, and a positive attitude create a pleasant environment in face-to-face communication.

- Open and transparent communication can overcome the lack of confidence, self-esteem, or fear of challenge to authority.
- An open mind and focus on listening to the entire message.
- To address differences in gender, educational level, emotions, beliefs, cultures, and values, avoid distrust and judgement.
- Show patience and respect, and consider seeking assistance from a translator to ensure accurate language and expressions. Avoid using jargon, complex words, and technical terms whenever possible.
- In principle, the safest way to address barriers is to ask the listener to give feedback. To avoid misinterpretations, the speaker should intimate assumptions, if any, in advance.
- When presenting large amounts of information, provide a summary at the end to highlight the key points and maintain focus.
- For individuals from Tier-2 and Tier-3 cities and villages, maintaining high standards of grammatically correct English may be challenging. Using simple, clear, and concise language, along with supportive apps, will be highly beneficial for them.
- Simple errors in emails can be corrected by sending a polite apology via email. For more serious mistakes, it is important to call the relevant person to offer both a verbal and written apology without any conditions. Corrections should be made promptly, accurately, and unconditionally.
- The message should be sent through appropriate channels to ensure early feedback from the recipient. Sensitive information should be sent through a secure medium like encrypted email.
- Organising regular training and refresher courses will go a long way in maintaining desirable standards.

Performance Enhancement

15

Communication Through Mobile Phones

Mobile communication occurs when two people interact via a mobile device. Mobile calls are the next best option for a face-to-face meeting. They provide flexibility in seeking information, are instantaneous, save time, offer instant feedback, and serve as great equalisers. These calls are particularly useful for developing and maintaining relationships over long distances.

In such interactions, it is crucial to remember that a real person is on another end of the line. Always maintain the highest level of courtesy, regardless of the individual's position or state of mind. Ensure that it is a convenient time for them before beginning the conversation.

To make the most of mobile communication, bear the following points in mind:

- Do not answer calls if you are eating, chewing gum, or working on your laptop. Likewise, it is impolite to take a call when during a meeting. The call will be logged as a 'Missed Call', which you can return later.

- Commit fully to the caller and give them your undivided attention. Do not interrupt if they have not finished speaking.
- While mobile conversations lack non-verbal cues, you can make up for this by modulating your voice. The notable exception is the smile: 'Even if people can't see you smiling, they can hear it.'
- Speak with positive energy, clarity, and warmth in a friendly, informal tone. Your business friends will appreciate your calls and engage with you for longer.
- Speaking in a monotone conveys disinterest, while slurring or mumbling can confuse the listener. Clear articulation, with the correct emphasis and variation in your tone, earns authority and respect.
- Remember that people also need time to think on the telephone, so do not feel obliged to fill every gap.
- In mobile interactions, concise answers work best.
- Summarise your conversation at the end of the call, especially in business discussions.
- Avoid becoming a slave of your mobile:
  - ✓ Create a 'mobile-free' zone for at least two hours daily for work calls, and let people know that you will call back later. For this, you can record a message. Refrain from checking WhatsApp messages during this time.
  - ✓ Make calls with a clear purpose; keep your social calls at work brief.
  - ✓ Resist the urge to check your mobile every time you receive a notification. Each distraction can cost you 30–50 seconds of focus.

16

Communication in Emails

Business emails have replaced written communications except where there is a legal requirement. They are used internally and externally to write plans, send job applications, schedule meetings, request information, explain matters, follow up, or send reminders. Therefore, every business email must have a specific purpose and a clear, actionable message. The email should be designed to easily elicit a response.

Given the critical role of emails in business communications, they should be drafted with care and sensitivity. This involves paying attention to each component of an email:

Addressee:

Ensure you correctly enter or copy the email address of the addressee. Double-check to avoid mistakes.

Mention in the body of the email if you are marking a copy to another person.

Subject Line:

The subject line is the first thing your recipient will see in their inbox. A strong subject line captures their attention and encourages them to read the entire message. In marketing emails, the subject line can be the deciding factor between the email being opened or deleted.

To achieve this, the subject line should be:

a. Clear and attention-grabbing.
b. Indicative that the email has originated from a secure source.
c. Relevant to the recipient, such as a deadline for a deliverable, approval of your new project idea, or a quarterly report. Preferably, each email should focus on one topic.

Salutation:

A formal business email should begin with 'Dear' followed by the recipient's name. Using 'Mr' or 'Ms' is recommended in your first email to the person. 'Hi' is acceptable for colleagues.

Greetings:

A brief, friendly greeting can set a positive tone, such as: 'It was great meeting you' or 'I enjoyed our recent chat'.

Request:

Within the first few lines, indicate the purpose of the email, e.g., 'I am writing to request an in-person meeting with you to explain our offer in detail'. For a job inquiry, mention the position and where you found the listing.

Body:

Be concise and to the point while ensuring all necessary information is included, whether it is a question, a request, an answer, or an explanation. Concise emails lead to quicker responses. Using bullet points, highlighting key information, or using a bold font can make the email more readable. Spacing out paragraphs also improves readability.

Closing:

Conclude the email by restating the desired action, the method of action (e.g., email or an in-person meeting), other contacts to be looped in and the deadline.

Email Attachments

If you are including an attachment, mention it in the body of the email and explain its purpose. Sending an attachment without context can confuse the recipient.

Sign-off:

A sign-off is essential. Use professional salutations like Regards, Sincerely, Warm Regards, Best Wishes, Thank You, or Thanks & Regards.

Signature:

Include your full name in the signature. Avoid initials, nicknames, or just your first name in professional emails. An automatic signature containing your full name, title, address, and mobile number adds a formal touch.

Important Tips

A cordial but urgent professional tone conveys your attitude and emotions about the subject or topic. In emails, your choice of words, punctuation, and sentence structure convey the same vocal tone and body language you would use in a face-to-face meeting.

To determine the appropriate tone, consider the nature of your audience, the purpose of your writing, and the key takeaway for the recipient. Elements such as humour, references to a mutual friend, flattery, seeking advice, issuing a mild challenge, or setting a deadline for a benefit can all influence the tone

However, a casual and curt tone can send the wrong impression. Avoid using informal, overly light-hearted, frivolous, or sarcastic tones. Additionally, refrain from casual language, run-on sentences, nonstandard grammar, slang, informal greetings, emojis, or unnecessary digressions.

Use Standard Fonts

Stick to standard, predictable fonts like Times New Roman, Arial, or Helvetica. These professional fonts will appear correctly in any browser or device.

Follow Up

After sending an email, allow at least 24 hours before following up.

Similarly, respond to emails you receive within 24 hours. This rule extends to phone calls and other forms of communication. Prompt responses show that you value the recipient's time.

Autoreply

Before going on holiday, set an autoresponder to inform senders that you are away and specify when you will return. Provide a colleague's contact details for urgent matters.

Common Email Mistakes

- Before you hit send, proofread your email to ensure it contains no errors, typos, spelling, or grammatical mistakes. Check the spelling of the recipient's name. Don't send anything you wouldn't want to be read aloud to you. Email mistakes can be costly.

- Emails are for communicating information, not for a conversation or a dialogue.
- Avoid letting emotions influence your writing, especially when you are upset. Sharing sensitive or personal via email is never secure—emails can be intercepted, screenshotted, downloaded, or printed.
- Avoid unprofessional signoffs such as Love (inappropriate), Thx or Rgds (childish), Take Care (overly casual), Looking forward to hearing from you (you better respond), Yours truly (old English), Respectfully/Respectfully yours (antique), Have a blessed day (religious overtones).
- With such heavy email traffic, it is human to make mistakes. Simple ones are nicknames, misspelt names, typo-filled messages, passive-aggressive tones, or unfinished drafts. Serious ones are Emails sent to the wrong addressee, replies to all or sharing a password, or annoying messages (casual tone, unwanted language, or words).
- If you make a mistake in an email, send a follow-up email, apologising and correcting the errors. Be prompt and accurate in your corrections.
- For more serious mistakes, call the concerned person and offer an unconditional verbal and written apology.

Remember, writing emails is a skill that improves with practice. You can learn best practices by observing the styles and methods of others.

17

Communication in Interviews

An interview is a crucial communication event where the interviewer seeks to gather information about your qualifications, skills, and personality to assess your suitability for a job, role, or position in an organisation. It goes beyond your CV, enabling the interviewer to gauge traits such as confidence, enthusiasm, passion, credibility, trustworthiness, resilience, and creativity.

An interview is an excellent opportunity to showcase your influencing skills and to persuade the interviewer that you are the best person for the job. Prepare examples of situations where you used these skills to achieve measurable outcomes.

The following tips will help you leave a lasting impression during the interview:

1. *The Organisation*: Research the organisation to identify some talking points or questions you can ask—it is the norm. Understand its strengths and challenges. Relate the job role to your experience and explain how you can add

value to the company. Express enthusiasm for the role and your desire to work for them. If your expertise lies in another area, explain why you are seeking a change and outline your preferences.

2. *Key Considerations*: Your behaviour, alertness, and non-verbal communication skills play a significant role in shaping the outcome of the interview.
3. *The First Impression*: Dress appropriately for the occasion, arrive early, and offer a firm handshake. A cheerful, energetic, professional demeanour and relaxed posture will create a positive first impression.
4. *Etiquette*: Be polite, honest, and concise. Thank the interviewers for their time to convey a positive attitude. Only use the interviewer's first name if explicitly invited to do so.
5. *Experience*: When asked about managing specific situations, this is your chance to highlight your skills such as commitment, perseverance, risk-taking ability and problem-solving. Provide concrete examples of how you excelled or overcame challenges.
6. *Confidence*: While confidence in your abilities is important, self-promotion is essential in persuading the interviewer that you are the right choice for the role. The interviewer will look for qualities that will help the organisation:
   - Do you work smart, rather than just hard?
   - Do you maintain a positive outlook, even in adversity?
   - Are you a collaborative, empathic team player?
   - Are you passionate about your work?
   - Are you a risk-taker who views failure as a learning opportunity?
   - Can you lead, but also follow when required?
   - Are you proactive and ready to deliver immediate results?

Speaking enthusiastically conveys your persuasive and negotiation skills, prompt decisions, and collaborative ability.

7. *Communication Skills*: An interview is an opportunity to build rapport with the interviewer and convince them you are a good fit for the company. When verbal language and body language align, the message becomes more powerful.
   - *Eye Contact*: An occasional warm smile and friendly expression with sincerity help put the interviewer at ease and build rapport.
   - *Listening*: Listen attentively to everything the interviewer says. This will help you respond appropriately and ask relevant questions. It also shows respect for the interviewer and enthusiasm for the organisation.
   - *Articulation*: Take a moment to gather your thoughts before answering a question. Articulating with clarity and respect showcases your skills, experience, confidence, and achievements. Be concise and use industry-specific terms to show your profound knowledge. Also, take steady breaths to maintain composure and clarity.

8. *Learn to Say No*: If you do not know the answer to a question, be honest. Express your willingness to learn, and develop your knowledge and skills—no one is expected to be perfect. Similarly, if the job does not excite you, it is better to decline politely than to regret your decision later.
9. *Ask Them Questions*: It is perfectly acceptable to ask questions about the organisation's culture, management style and operations. You are entitled to find out if the organisation is the right fit for you.

10. *Salary Expectations*: Be clear about the salary range you are willing to accept. You should also be prepared to explain the reason for the salary increase in the previous job.
11. *Avoid*:
    - Avoid yawning or appearing distracted, and refrain from fidgeting or exhibiting other nervous behaviours.
    - Do not over-communicate; good communication is often concise. A light touch of humour is acceptable, but jokes should be avoided, as interviews are serious business.
    - Do not interrupt while the interviewer is speaking, and do not exaggerate your responses. They have called you because they are interested in your profile—maintain a positive attitude throughout.
    - Avoid slang, colloquialisms, rambling or talking too fast, or using fillers such as 'you know', 'uh', or 'like'.
    - Looking down at your shoes or other objects in the room conveys your apprehension and nerves.

12. *Practice*: Practice interviewing with a friend or family member or in front of a mirror. Rehearsing builds self-confidence and enthusiasm and helps you relax in the interview.
13. *Post-interview*: Send a thank-you email within twenty-four hours of the interview, expressing gratitude for the opportunity. Mention the interview date and time and affirm your interest in the position. If appropriate, indicate your interest in a follow-up interview.

    If you are no longer interested in the position, politely ask to be removed from the candidate pool without burning your bridges.

If the decision date has passed, follow up with a phone call or email to check your status. Reaffirm your interest in the position, and offer any additional information they may need.

If you do not receive an offer, send a thank you email, reiterating your interest in future opportunities.

If you receive an offer but decide to decline, send an email to graciously decline the position, explaining the reason for your decision. Keep the communication lines open for the future.

14. *Key Takeaways*: After the interview, take note of what went well and what did not. This reflection will help you improve for future interviews.

18

Teachers' Communication

Teachers use one-way communication in the pedagogical learning format to educate children and young learners. The students' responses are mainly non-verbal. The teaching profession has mastered this challenging communication skill to manage the delivery environment.

As an educator, the teacher lays the foundation for the growth of the students—academically, emotionally, and socially—to become leaders, entrepreneurs, social activists, and professionals. Teaching, therefore, is considered one of the greatest professions that contribute to the healthy growth of society, nation, and the world.

However, no skill sets make a great teacher—you must be in love with yourself and proud of the profession for contributing to developing young minds year after year and the opportunities it provides for a fulfilling life. A bit of creativity and out-of-the-box thinking can bring a lot of fun to your chosen career.

Teachers are important links in maintaining open and transparent communication among themselves, their parents, colleagues, and the administration. Thus, they must acquire super communication skills and work on their attitudes and mindsets.

Some of the challenges before them are:

1. *Composition of the Class*: Students have different learning abilities, styles, backgrounds, and parents' expectations. They are different, with unique strengths, weaknesses, and interests. They may be uncomfortable seeking help and sharing their needs, struggles, and triumphs. Not all students are good at academics. It is not right to expect them to learn at the same pace. Classrooms with large populations add to their woes.

   These challenges offer valuable opportunities for teachers to enhance their communication and creative skills. By treating students with love and empathy, teachers can foster a positive and supportive atmosphere where emotional needs are met. Being friendly, approachable, and accessible helps students feel comfortable expressing themselves without fear of judgement or ridicule. Address issues such as apathy, misbehaviour, bullying, low attendance, non-participation, and missed homework with care and attention.
2. *Disciplining students*: Disciplining students is a massive challenge in the classroom and can be emotionally disturbing and draining for both teachers and students.

   Be a positive example they can admire and trust. Treat them fairly. Share your life experiences to encourage them to improve their behaviour.

   Ask students about their goals and aspirations and encourage them to pursue knowledge, technology, hobbies, and sports after classes. This will improve their learning experience, and invigorate creativity, curiosity, and passion for sports.

State your expectations clearly when assigning them tasks. Set disruption-dealing plans and be consistent in applying them. This will go a long way toward keeping the classrooms fully engaged, addressing anxiety, and bubbling with energy.

Make lessons interactive and hands-on, creating a safe and supportive environment through open dialogue. Connect the learning to its relevance in daily life to provide students with real-world experience.

Inspire students to be more self-directed. Delegate and ask for help. This will free up your time to focus on more significant tasks.

Creating an excellent personalised learning plan is a long-term process. However, it is worth the effort, as it gives students the best chance of success. Provide various learning experiences like research, experimentation, brainstorming, and group discussions.

3. *Getting Organised*: It is vital to take breaks throughout the day to clear your head and recharge. Otherwise, you will quickly feel overwhelmed and bogged down. Teachers should maintain flexible plans to avoid burnout and have backups ready when their schedule is disrupted. Regular exercise and meditation will help. They should also develop a good support system among peers, friends, and family members.

   Prioritise each student's individual needs and track their progress. This will help you stay on top and ensure no student falls through the cracks.

   When engaging students in activities, always prioritise their safety to avoid injuries. Experiment with different learning strategies to suit their abilities and levels of knowledge. Politeness, Patience, Perseverance and Assertiveness are hallmarks of a great teacher.

4. *Communication*: With high parents' expectations and demands from the administration, communication is a big issue in schools. Engage with parents positively and proactively—they are on your side. Respond promptly to their concerns via email, phone, or in person. Share the child's progress and alert them to any issues. Be proactive in maintaining open communication with administration and colleagues as well.
5. *Work-Life Balance*: With the pressure of completing the course on time, administrative work, school events, and functions, maintaining health and work-life balance can be challenging.

   Spending time on innovative lesson plans and field trips and leveraging apps for collaborative class management and data collection can help you manage your tasks.

   Sharpening your skills in communication, trust building, planning, teaching strategies, and school management will help you enhance your efficacy in the long term.

   To maintain health, follow an exercise regimen and participate in sports. By taking care of yourself, with a decent dose of 'Me Time,' you can manage the challenges and improve the quality of your life.

Teaching is the noblest profession in the world, but it is not for the faint-hearted. Staying with it through difficult times takes dedication, time, and grit.

19

Trainers' Communication

Typically, corporate trainers are involved in skilling, reskilling, and upskilling employees to enhance workplace efficiency in the long term. The training industry and the corporate world presume that the trainees will implement their new skills in the workplace. Unfortunately, working against deadlines, delivering against targets, and managing day-to-day crises sidelines this implementation.

The next challenge for corporates is the learning format used by the training industry. Corporate training is delivered to adults in a pedagogical format—the standard 'tell and expect' practice in child learning for imparting knowledge to children. However, this approach is not engaging enough to promote learning and implementation among adults.

Research has shown that adults are curious to know:

i. What should they learn?
ii. Why should they learn it?

iii. Whether it is of immediate value to them.
iv. Whether it will solve their problems.
v. Whether they will see the results they desire immediately.

The transfer of the 'gyan' method used in pedagogy is the least effective way of training adults in a corporate environment.

In the andragogy learning format, adults learn by sharing their experiences in a stress-free, enjoyable environment. By sharing with co-participants, they test their knowledge, remove doubts, validate their views, and clarify their thought processes.

The direct benefit is that learning becomes an internalised process, allowing individuals to take ownership—transforming them into self-learners who are oriented and motivated to learn. This sense of ownership fosters a growth mindset, where positive results motivate further efforts, and negative ones provide opportunities for learning and experimentation.

By sharing successes and failures, the classroom becomes abuzz with energising activities and excitement. The shame associated with failure dissipates, as it is accepted as a part of the journey.

Thus, implementation instils confidence in employees, cultivating an 'I CAN' attitude for success. They come to embrace failures as part of their journey, understanding that results materialise only when learning and moving on. They know that results happen only when learning is pursued with passion, enjoyment, and positivity.

From 'I Can', they progress to 'We Can', forming teams that drive organisational objectives. Human capital undergoes an Attitude Transformation and Mindset Change. Therefore, the most significant advantage of using andragogy is the immediate manifestation of Performance Enhancement at the individual or team levels during the training programme itself.

Andragogy is an experiential learning approach that encourages open communication and fosters team building. The trainer takes on the role of an active listener and 'Facilitator', reinforcing learning by sharing personal experiences.

Other pointers to improve pedagogical facilitation include:

- Timing, brevity, high energy, and enthusiasm enhance positivity in the classroom.
- Empathy, accuracy, clarity, courtesy, and active listening are essential.
- A trainer sharing stories and experiences tends to be more popular than a knowledgeable speaker delivering a monologue. Relevant games, activities, situational analysis, icebreakers, and key pointers add value to the subject and make learning enjoyable.
- Probing questions to remove doubts, such as 'Have I been clear?' or 'Do you want me to take you through this again?' are better options than asking, 'Do you understand?'
- A facilitator need not have all the answers; requesting time to revert is acceptable and not embarrassing. Instead, try saying, 'I don't know this; let's search for the information together.'
- A facilitator must be sensitive to the participants' non-verbal cues. They should also handle criticism and tough questions with maturity and humour. Ignoring minor mischief can enhance the enjoyable learning experience.
- It is okay to feel angry, but losing control is unacceptable. The facilitator must maintain composure in the face of distractions.
- A facilitator should be skilled in providing *constructive feedback*.

The Business

20

Communication in Team Building

It is widely acknowledged that two individuals working together achieve better results than individuals. With more people joining hands, outcomes improve quantitatively and qualitatively. A supportive nature and friendliness foster the understanding to bring out the best in teams.

The subject of team building has been extensively studied, researched, and written about, perhaps more widely and profoundly than any other topic in management. These studies have identified several factors influencing a team's effectiveness, the most critical being communication.

Communication is the key element of a team, to the point that communication and teamwork are inseparable.

- Communication within the team is built around the principles of ABC: Accuracy, Brevity (the KISS principle: keep it short and simple) and Clarity.
- Also, effective communication takes place from HEART:

H = Hear to understand.
E = Even if you disagree, do not prove others wrong.
A = Acknowledge greatness and appreciate others' points of view.
R = Recognise good intentions.
T = Tell the truth with compassion.

Teamwork does not happen by chance; it is a by-product of good communication within the team, which contributes to the growth and development of the team:

- 'I win when all those I work or interact with win'. Ask the other person, with humility, 'What can I do to help you win?' Be an 'I CAN' person (take charge) and empower those around you to become 'I CAN' people too.
- Always begin with the end in mind.
- This is crucial when communicating team goals (expectations, customer or internal). Visualising success enhances the team's motivation.
- Positive statements inspire pride, positivity, and energy. They encourage assertive behaviour and promote discussions about planning, coordination, improvements, and achievements.
- Success has many interpretations because everyone takes ownership of it. Any experience labelled as a success becomes a positive one, and vice versa. Start with positive thoughts and make even team achievements feel significant.
- Appreciate and applaud Winners: 'Excellent, you won!' 'What did you do right to achieve success?' or 'Who contributed the most to the victory?'
- Support those who fall short: 'With just a little more effort, you could have won.' 'How could you have won?' 'What did you do right?' or 'How did you get it right?'

- Negative questions elicit defensive responses. Those who did not succeed may avoid eye contact, shift blame to each other, or cite external factors such as tools or materials. Asking, 'Why did you lose badly?' or 'Who is responsible for the loss?' is the easiest way to demoralise the team—you will achieve nothing. Blame games lead nowhere.
- After losing a deal due to an unintended mistake, you feel disappointed. No one says a word, yet accusing faces surround you. The team behaves as though no one else has committed any blunders, let alone minor mistakes. In times of distress, we all need a shoulder to cry on and a hand to hold. Later, we will analyse the mishap to learn from it.
- In every project, whether it succeeds or fails, people will always do some things right and some things wrong. Failures are part of life's journey and offer invaluable learning experiences. Keep working on improvements and adding value each time. Every failure holds a lesson that can lead to success.
- Imagine returning excited after closing an important deal, only to be disappointed when your team does not applaud your effort or the leader does not acknowledge it. Many people quit their jobs because they feel unappreciated.
- Fostering a culture of empowerment helps maintain high team motivation.
- Practise open, transparent, and direct communication within the team (this applies to family members and friends as well):
- To minimise the natural loss of meaning in communication, speak directly with all concerned team members whenever possible. If communication passes through multiple layers, it can lead to distortion, confusion, chaos, and sometimes disasters.
- Remember the game of Chinese Whispers, where a verbal message passed along a chain of participants often ends

up as a completely different, sometimes absurd, version of the original.

- Direct communication can be tedious, time-consuming, and even painful, but it is essential for building an effective and efficient team.
- When communicating with a multi-layered team, issuing written directions down to the minutest detail—through a letter or email—is often the best approach.
- Feedback is crucial in building a powerful team. If a mistake is made, usually unintentionally, it must be reviewed.
- At times, strong words may be necessary to correct a mistake. However, the intent behind the feedback should always be to benefit and serve others, and it should be delivered as decently as possible. It is not what you say that hurts people, but 'how' you say it makes the difference.
- Sharing the rationale behind your feedback will soften the impact.
- Be sensitive to factors such as gender, personal space, territory, perceptions, environment, and organisational values.
- Be mindful of your contributions, actions, and reactions in a team context. The better you manage yourself, the stronger your team becomes. Every member, regardless of role, is responsible and accountable for the team's success.
- Direct, honest, and open communication—delivered with love, care, patience, humility, and empathy—builds trust, strengthens relationships, and fosters team bonding.
- Being honest about your weaknesses—without feeling threatened—allows the team to support you. Just as one odd thumb and four fingers form a powerful fist, you become a better team player, and the team emerges stronger.

- Share your strengths, skills, and abilities with your team, and your weaknesses will be balanced by others' strengths.
- While one or two key members may occasionally carry the load in a team, in a highly functional team, every member strives to contribute equally. For instance, in sports, it takes the entire team performing well to win. Success shines when each member handles their responsibilities efficiently. Avoid hogging the limelight.
- Do not hesitate to express your point if you feel strongly about it. If your idea is not accepted, consider putting it in writing to the entire team. Your suggestion might still be rejected, but you will have strengthened your credibility for future roles. Also, not all ideas are brilliant or right.
- Argue passionately, but once a decision is made, commit fully to its implementation—do not deceive your team.
- Keep a journal for recording your experiences. This will help you understand the connections between actions and results, and provide deeper insights into what makes an effective team builder. Learn from each other's mistakes to build and strengthen your team.

Group Dynamics

Managing a large team or a crowd is different from traditional team-building practices. Group Dynamics principles come into play when building cohesive teams:

- Decisions reached in group meetings may differ (for better or worse) from those made by individuals. This is due to exchange of ideas, experiences, coordination, agreements, and negotiations within the group.

- Articulate individuals who speak with conviction and authority (which is often more important than knowledge) naturally emerge as group leaders.
- If you do not participate in the discussions, your intelligence and knowledge are lost to the group. If you are in a leadership role, it is vital to seek input from all group members.
- When addressing a complex issue, do not hesitate to accept input from an observer or a witness who may not be directly involved in the discussion. You never know which idea, from which source, will prove valuable.

The discussion above establishes a direct link between communication and team building—you cannot build an effective team without mastering communication skills.

Train continuously and regularly to enhance team performance and address communication issues. Remember, each team member is unique, and there are no set rules or practices to apply.

Some pointers would help:

Issue	Solution
They do not know what to do.	Train them in detail on their roles, Key Result Areas, and your expectations.
They do not have the required equipment.	Equip them.
They do not know how to attend to their tasks.	Demonstrate how to deliver. Follow it up with mentoring till they are comfortable in the process.
They are not allowed to act.	Cut the red tape.

Issue	Solution
They are not willing to act.	Help establish, 'What is in it for me.' Provide motivational inputs.
They are not delivering consistently.	Guide, mentor, and audit till they start delivering consistently.
They still are not delivering.	Try once more and if they still do not deliver, look for fresh talent. Ducks cannot fly like pigeons.

21

Communications in Meetings

A meeting is a simple, time-saving decision-making management process involving two or more people working together to accomplish a specific task. Complex issues involving contradictory views are referred to in a meeting. A meeting may also be called to pass on information about a complex issue and to explain its implications.

Meetings are classified into three categories: One-to-one (interviews), One-to-a-few (office meetings) and One-to-many (public meetings). Here, we are discussing the one-to-a-few meetings. The other two categories have been discussed in earlier Chapters.

One-to-a-few meetings aim to arrive at a joint decision, consensus, or agreement on a plan of action. They are labelled as task force meetings, board meetings, committee meetings, progress reviews in a large project, team performance reviews, or planning meetings.

To organise a productive and time-efficient meeting, it is best to follow a structure:

1. **Purpose:**
   Before planning a meeting, it is vital to identify its purpose and intended outcome. The convener should answer the following questions:
   - Is the meeting necessary?
   - What is the desired outcome?
   - Is the meeting the best way to achieve the outcome?
   - Is the meeting the best way to achieve the outcome?
   - Are there alternative methods, such as a Zoom call, conference call, written communication, or email?

2. **Participants:**
   The convener identifies the invitees who will contribute to the meeting's outcome.

   Invite people from various fields and diverse expertise to ensure that all the relevant points of view are represented. However, the list should be restricted to only those who can contribute meaningfully to the decision-making process, have the authority to make decisions, and carry out the decisions. Check the critical invitees' availability before fixing the meeting date and time.

3. **Agenda:**
   The convener normally sets the agenda or invites the participants to forward suggestions. To ensure a timely and successful meeting conclusion, include only relevant, essential issues that the group has the authority to address. Include notes explaining the dimensions of each issue, purpose, and desired outcomes.

   Having a single-point agenda is the best for holding a focused meeting. However, it may not always be feasible, such as in board meetings involving multiple related issues or outstation attendees.

The agenda should be circulated sufficiently in advance to allow participants time to prepare for the discussion and make decisions quickly.

4. **Duration**

   The agenda will determine the meeting's duration.

   Participants should be informed of the meeting's duration, ideally alongside the agenda, so they can factor it into their schedules and travel plans.

5. **Meeting Site**

   The meeting should be held in a room that comfortably accommodates the invitees, allowing everyone to face each other. If refreshments or audio-visual equipment are needed, they should be arranged in advance.

6. **Conduct of a Meeting**

   To ensure a positive and effective outcome, the leader should consider the following:

   - Assign the task of recording minutes to one of the attendees or ask a scribe.
   - Arrive early, and start and end on time. If the agenda cannot be completed, defer unfinished items to another meeting.
   - If not all members are familiar with each other, ask attendees to introduce themselves.
   - All members should be treated with the same respect. The leader should foster a win-win atmosphere, allow differences of opinion to be aired with a positive spirit, and approach others' views with an open mind.
   - Do not rush; move the meeting along with well-timed summaries once a decision has arrived.

- Start each agenda item with a discussion and invite members to offer their comments, inputs, and questions.
- Discourage disruptions such as the use of mobile phones, side conversations, and discussions of topics not on the agenda.
- Meeting minutes should be circulated as soon as possible to ensure prompt action.

Group Dynamics

Several studies have shown that a group's decisions can differ from those made by individuals, and these decisions can be better or worse.

A person who is articulate or speaks with authority may dominate the discussion, even if they are not the most knowledgeable member of the group.

It is the leader's responsibility to consult all participants, particularly those who have been reluctant to contribute. You never know who might offer the best idea that will work.

22

The Elephant in the Room

You are sitting in the conference room, minding your business, and waiting for the meeting to start. Suddenly, a grey 10,000-pound trunk-swinging monstrosity enters. To the dismay of all present, it plants itself firmly in the centre of the room. Everyone knows the problem, but it is so sensitive that nobody dares acknowledge its existence. Without a word being uttered, everybody decides to ignore it.

The meeting begins and concludes. As expected, everyone is so distracted that they only vaguely remember what was discussed.

We have all experienced 'the elephant in the room' phenomenon, where everyone avoids deciding on a sensitive issue even though it has serious consequences. Discussing it will foster fear, consume time, and impede productivity. It will disturb the status quo and is best left alone. Everybody involved believes and hopes the issue will be resolved in due time.

However, a leader or management cannot shirk the responsibility. It must be addressed head-on to contain its damaging effects. If no one is willing to act, the elephant in the room presents an opportunity for you to demonstrate your leadership skills.

In the first instance, verify that it is real and exists. Recognising the issue's existence is an essential step. It helps create an enabling environment to accept and discuss it openly. By naming what everyone avoids, you will transform the elephant into a surmountable obstacle not distorted by perception.

Present it to your team now to gain their acceptance of the issue that must be addressed. You are challenging your team, demonstrating respect for their capabilities. This will establish your leadership quality, showing that you have the confidence to solve a difficult problem together.

Looking into its genesis—what caused it first—may provide a clue to finding a doable solution. Define its contour, size, and colour to check the gaps and missing pieces. Now, we have a somewhat known demon to deal with.

Check if some of the segments of the issue can be resolved. It would save time in the long run. Devising foolproof strategies for the whole can be time-consuming and counterproductive. Start small and develop strategies as you go along—one step at a time—like a stream trying to find its path.

Be mindful of emotions and allow open communication, even if the issue is unpleasant. Tiptoeing around even minor aspects of the issue will only perpetuate the tension.

Open the discussion, giving others a chance to contribute. This shows consideration for their perspective, creates focus, and provides an opportunity to discuss a once 'forbidden' subject. It also prevents it from reverting to 'elephant' status.

Before the meeting concludes, be sure everyone understands the issue, discusses all its facets, and answers all questions. They should be confident they have a clear plan and ideas of what to do next.

The elephant in the room has taken a distinguishable shape and contour.

23

Communication in Presentations

A presentation is a powerful tool for communicating your thoughts and ideas to an audience in various speaking situations (group, meeting, or briefing). It could be informative for imparting knowledge or have a 'persuasive' angle, like a deal, a sale, or seeking funds for a project.

Some pointers are universal for preparing an informative and impactful presentation:

- Keep both the presentation and slides simple.
- The purpose, goal, and outcome should be stated clearly to establish its relevance to the audience. List them in the beginning and at the end.
- Create an exciting structure. An exciting opening will hook the audience instantly. Embellish the presentation with compelling stories and experiences.
- A well-prepared and practised presentation will enhance your confidence level.

- Practice verbal and non-verbal communication skills to make an impact. The focus on the latter—a smiling face, friendly body language, and eye contact—will create a more lasting impression.
- A memorable closing will stay with the audience longer.

Creating an impactful presentation requires careful planning, attention to detail and a good eye for design:

The Purpose: Identify the purpose of the presentation—the occasion, the subject, its scope, the context, the message you wish to convey, the composition and the audience size. Know your audience's language, interests, expectations, and challenges to connect easily with them.

Other relevant factors are the duration of the presentation, place, and delivery time (e.g., a small room with natural light, an informal setting, or a vast lecture room lit with stage lights), setting of the presentation (formal or informal, a stage or a board room), and availability of the equipment.

If you are unfamiliar with the location and setting, visiting in advance or arriving early to familiarise yourself would be advantageous.

Research your Topic: To make an impactful presentation, you must research your topic thoroughly. Identify stories, experiences, and bonus information you want to share.

The Content: A significant body to provide the details, the logic, and the supporting evidence to support your opening statement. It should be clear, concise, creative, credible, authentic, full of value, and easily understandable. Have a worthwhile narrative, gift-wrap your talk, and its flavour will linger for a long time.

To support your content, you must include data and statistics—charts, graphs, and maps. Share stories, experiences, and practical examples to make a direct connection. To make the slides captivating, add multimedia, such as photos, graphics, videos, GIFs, or audio narrations.

The Presentation: Your first impression is extremely important in setting the stage for the rest of your talk.

- Pay attention to your attire and the picture you present.
- Start with a hook, personal story, provocative statement, surprising fact, question, prop, visual or video.
- Initially, introduce yourself to establish your credentials, build trust, and create a positive impression.
- Your core presentation should last half the designated time—the rest must be reserved for sharing stories, experiences, bonus information, and Q&A. However, do not close with a Q&A session; to involve the audience, encourage them to ask questions throughout the presentation.
- Summarise the presentation at the end and use a strong 'Call to Action,' emphasising your main point.

Slides Design

Your presentation's delivery will influence the flow of slides.

- While designing the slides, keep them clutter-free and brief. Communication ceases when the speaker or the audience is not in eye-to-eye contact.
- To keep the audience engaged, restrict the 24-point font text on each slide to 4–6 lines. Use punchy phrases to minimise the text. Presenting 10 such slides takes about 20 minutes. The best slide contains only one word or an expression, and the rest is the story woven around it, delivered by you verbally.
- Use a white background and no more than two fonts to give the presentation a polished and professional look. Bring in variations by playing with the weight, styling,

colours (no more than two), and size of the fonts. Follow the same pattern in all slides to keep it visually pleasing. If required, fonts and colours should maintain your company's visual identity.

- Use 36–40 font size for the headings and 24–28 for the text to ensure the audience keeps the focus on the presenter.
- Animated transitions between slides can make your presentation more engaging. However, use only one transition style for your entire presentation to keep everything cohesive.
- To keep your design sleek and uncluttered, it is best to have one main idea or one takeaway per slide. You could also use a simple image and lines or tables to provide visual cues to the presentation.
- This Presenter's Notes feature, appearing at the bottom of the PPT, uses keeping notes for the presenter without sacrificing a smart slide design. These notes will pop up as needed when you are presenting, and you can open them on your computer screen while showing a particular slide.

Once you have the rough draft of your presentation ready, proofread it several times to ensure:

- The presentation sticks to your central message.
- The sequence of the slides is correct (crucial).
- Unnecessary or irrelevant information is deleted.
- The slides are less cluttered and more visually pleasing.
- Grammatical errors are eliminated (use apps).
- Stories and experiences you wish to share are identified.
- You edit and rehearse at intervals, loudly, and with a timer to aid memory retention. Seek the help of your team.
- Recording and listening to yourself boosts overnight retention.

Rehearse & Memorise Your Presentation.

Memorise your presentation for a natural delivery. Weave in your stories, experiences, and clarification of doubts.

Some additional pointers to help:

- Associate concepts and ideas with specific situations.
- Write essential points in the notes to remember information more efficiently.
- Memorisation with awareness (understanding every word) is vital to sharp memory.

The Delivery

The Expectations: Success in a presentation is about meeting the audience's expectations. Creating an engaging narration reflecting your thoughts is vital.

The Delivery: Remember, people buy people first, and then they do business. How you say is more critical than what you say. You are offering a story, an experience, an emotional journey.

You deliver a message verbally, but your appearance, demeanour, non-verbal communication skills and visual aids will determine its impact:

Mode	Voice Control	Body Language	Content
Lengthy presentation	45%	40%	15%
Short (1–2 minutes)	38%	55%	7%

Successful presenters are authentic, even imperfect. Instead of hiding their insecurities, they own them and build an emotional connect. The best is to use a conversational style and be yourself.

Words delivered with certainty, firm voice, enthusiasm, variety, and pitch add energy to the room.

Wear business formals with a smile, stand tall and relaxed, chin up and maintain eye contact to make the delivery appear natural.

Keep the focus on YOU and your narration, not the PowerPoint. The slides are just aids. Move gently if you wish to move around, but never turn your back to your audience.

Jargon, negative comments, swaying, leaning on a chair, or using the slides as a teleprompter should be avoided.

Observe Audience Behaviour

Your presentation is not a one-way street; you are having a dialogue. Your effectiveness is reflected by the audience's expressions, body language, and questions. Fidgeting, yawning, or looking at phones conveys that they are bored. Ask a question, make them laugh, change the subject, or do an activity to bring them back into the room.

Video Presentations

Delivery of presentations over the Internet such as Zoom or Team, would require different strategies to meet the challenges:

- Make delivery at higher pitch and energy levels to address local distractions and low attention.
- Keep the presentations shorter and crisper by summarising the text on each slide—they are reading it directly.
- Allow more space for asking questions on both sides to avoid boredom.

Impediments and Backup Plans

Avoid information, text, or data overload.

In addition to your preparation, have backup plans to handle exigencies such as location change, background noise, excessively warm or cool rooms, distractions, technical difficulties, and power failures.

It all starts by choosing a great topic. If you cannot choose a favourite topic, find a unique angle, such as focusing on a specific problem.

Finally, there is no shortcut to rehearsing well to overcome your fear of public speaking.

Make a Beginning

Relax, take a breath, and enjoy the moment. Nerves are normal; the audience wants *you to* succeed.

24

Communication in Conflicts

Conflicts arise whenever there are disagreements in opinions or interests in human interaction. They can occur between two or more employees, managers, or team members, as well as between producers or service providers and clients in the marketplace. In personal contexts, conflicts may arise within families or society at large.

Conflicts can begin as minor disagreements or debates and escalate into intense confrontations. Various factors contribute to these conflicts, including differing personalities, perspectives, suppressed feelings, unresolved past issues, competing interests, uncertainty regarding roles and responsibilities, jockeying for positions, clashing personalities, limited time and resources, and fragile egos. While we may share the same goals, we often have differing views on how to achieve them.

Most disputes are resolved through negotiations or third-party intervention. However, it is crucial to address conflicts before they escalate into unhealthy tensions, as they can negatively impact productivity, relationships, morale, and teamwork.

The ability to resolve conflicts is often regarded as a leadership quality. People who can identify conflicts, acknowledge different opinions, and build consensus are highly valuable in organisations.

Developing conflict resolution skills requires time and practice, with the fundamental issue often being a lack of open and transparent communication. Although this analysis focuses on workplace conflicts, the approach can be effectively applied in other contexts.

Conflict resolution is essential at the workplace to:

- Find peaceful solutions to everyday challenges and utilise valuable resources such as time, energy, reputation, and motivation more effectively.
- Address underlying issues arising from participants' diverse backgrounds, ideas, and beliefs.
- Foster team cohesion, alleviate discontent, promote open communication, and cultivate a collaborative work environment.
- Maintain low-stress levels across the board, making it easier to focus and engage with the conflicting parties.
- Enhance efficiency among opposing parties by directing attention toward goals rather than disputes.
- Retain the skills and knowledge of experienced employees.

Conflict resolution begins by acknowledging its existence. While no one enjoys conflict, it can be tempting to ignore it or assume it will resolve itself. Thus, it is important to address it amicably and promptly, as unresolved conflicts can spread like wildfire.

The process of conflict resolution starts by identifying a mediator. This mediator could be the organisation's manager, a senior management official, or the CEO. Alternatively, the organisation may choose to appoint an external mediator.

The mediator's role includes:

1. Finding a safe and neutral location to discuss the conflict, ensuring the environment is free from interruptions to facilitate direct, open, and honest communication.
2. Understanding the conflict and defining the problem: who is involved, what caused it, and each side's perspective, concerns, and positions, approached with empathy and patience. This may require several rounds of interaction with the affected parties and others. Understanding the underlying issue not only aids in resolving the current conflict but also helps prevent future occurrences.
3. Actively listening to both sides of the story while keeping the discussion focused, respectful, and reasonable. Encourage open dialogue until both sides recognise each other's perspectives, needs, and feelings, setting aside their differences and preferences. It is crucial to avoid personal emotions and attachment to a specific side.
4. Initiating thorough investigations—free from prejudices and assumptions—to understand each position, underlying conflict, its source, and severity.
5. If multiple parties (witnesses and all concerned stakeholders) are involved, invite them into an open communication environment. Ask them to share their views, perceptions, feelings, conflict causes, and possible solutions in alignment with organisational objectives. Discuss each idea thoroughly.
6. Consider what else might be involved and who else could be consulted. If an idea is not acceptable, discuss the reasons why.

7. Once the basic facts have been clarified, use a collaborative approach, urging both parties to listen to one another's perspectives to arrive at a mutually acceptable solution and action plan. Encourage open expression of views, even during disagreements, as silence from one or more parties may indicate resistance.

Strategies to effectively negotiate conflicts:

- Set ground rules, such as encouraging each side to use "I" statements and avoid "You" statements, which imply blame.
- Be an active listener and remain patient, demonstrating attentiveness. Maintain professionalism and impartiality in all interactions to earn and preserve the respect of both sides.
- Keep exploring until the sources of conflict are identified.
- Recognise when to take a break if emotions are running high or tensions need to be eased.
- Prepare for and engage in difficult conversations.
- Work collaboratively to resolve the conflict while also repairing relationships.
- The mediator should be mindful of their body language to avoid inadvertently conveying messages. To project sincerity, calmness, and open-mindedness:
  - Maintain eye contact.
  - Be aware of your facial expressions.
  - Relax your neck and shoulders.
  - Use a neutral tone, speaking at a moderate speed and volume.
  - Frame positive statements.
  - Avoid absolute terms like 'always' or 'never'.

25

Communication in Negotiations

Negotiation involves a back-and-forth communication process to reach an agreement acceptable to two (or more) sides from various options, to where both parties contribute. Typically, participants enter negotiations perceiving themselves as competitors, convinced, 'I will win easily; I am on the right side, holding all the cards.' This assumption is one-sided, as the other side's facts are unknown.

Successful negotiations that yield satisfactory outcomes for both sides emerge when three stages are followed:

1. Identifying the facts from both sides.
2. Exploring possible solutions.
3. Determining the best solution.

To clarify this approach, let us examine the following case study of the Ugli Orange:

A. Role of Roland

Your name is Dr P.W. Roland. You work as a research biologist for a pharmaceutical firm. The firm is under contract with the government to research methods to combat enemy uses of biological warfare.

Recently, several World War II experimental nerve gas bombs were moved from the U.S. to a small island just off the U.S. coast in the Pacific. In the process of transporting them, two of the bombs developed a leak. The lead is presently controlled, but government scientists believe that the gas will permeate the bomb chambers within two weeks. They know no method of preventing the gas from getting into the atmosphere and spreading to other islands. Several thousands of people will likely incur serious brain damage or die.

You've developed a synthetic vapour that will neutralise nerve gas if it is injected into the bomb chamber before the gas leaks out. The vapour is made with a chemical taken from the rind of the rare Ugli orange. Unfortunately, only 4000 of these oranges were produced this season.

You've been informed, on good evidence, that R.H. Cardoza, a fruit exporter in South America, has 3000 Ugli oranges. The chemicals from the rinds of this number of oranges would be enough to neutralise the gas if the serum is developed and injected efficiently. You have also been informed that the rinds of these oranges are in good condition.

You have also been informed that Dr J.W. Jones is urgently seeking the purchase of Ugli oranges, and s/he is also aware of R.H. Cardoza's possession of the 3000 available. Dr Jones works for a firm with which your firm is highly competitive. There is a great deal of industrial espionage in the pharmaceutical industry. Over the years, your firm and Dr Jones have sued each other for violations of industrial espionage laws and infringement of patent rights several times. Litigation on two suits is still being processed. The Federal government has asked your firm for assistance.

You've been authorised by your firm to approach R.H. Cardoza to purchase the 3000 Ugli oranges. You have been told they will sell them to the highest bidder. Your firm has authorised you to bid as high as $250,000 to obtain the rind of the oranges.

Before approaching R.H. Cardoza, you decide to talk to Dr Jones to influence her/him so that s/he will not prevent you from purchasing the oranges.

B. Role for Jones

You are Dr J. W. Jones, a biological research scientist employed by a pharmaceutical firm.

You have recently developed a synthetic chemical useful for curing and preventing Rudosen. Rudosen is a disease contracted by pregnant women. If not caught in the first four weeks of pregnancy, the disease causes serious brain, eye, and ear damage to the unborn child.

Recently, there has been an outbreak of Rudosen in your state, and several thousand women have contracted the disease. You have found, with volunteer victims, that your recently developed synthetic serum cures Rudosen in its early stages. Unfortunately, the serum is from Ugli orange juice, a rare fruit. Only a small quantity (approximately 4000) of these oranges were produced last season. No additional Ugli oranges will be available until next season, which will be too late to cure the present Rudosen victims.

You've demonstrated that your synthetic serum is not harmful to pregnant women, and there are no side effects. The Food and Drug Administration has approved the production and distribution of the serum as a cure for Rudosen. Unfortunately, the present outbreak was unexpected, and your firm had not planned on having the compound serum available for six months. Your firm holds patents on synthetic serums, and they are expected to be highly profitable products when they are generally available to the public.

On good evidence, you have recently been informed that R.H. Cardoza, a South American fruit exporter, has 3000 Ugli oranges in good condition. If you could obtain the juice of all 3000, you would be able to cure the present victims and provide enough inoculation for the remaining pregnant women in the state. No other state currently has a Rudosen threat.

You have recently been informed that Dr P.W. Roland is also urgently seeking Ugli oranges and is aware of R.H. Cardoza's possession of the 3000 available. Dr Roland is employed by a competitor pharmaceutical firm. S/he has been working on biological warfare research for the past several years. There is a great deal of industrial espionage in the pharmaceutical industry. Over the past several years, Dr Roland and your firm have sued each other for infringement of patent rights and espionage law violations several times.

You've been authorised by your firm to approach R.H. Cardoza to purchase the 3000 Ugli oranges. You have been told s/he will sell them to the highest bidder. Your firm has authorised you to bid as high as $250,000 to obtain the juice of the 3000 available oranges.

Before approaching R.H. Cardoza, you decide to talk with Dr Roland to influence her/him so that s/he will not prevent you from purchasing the oranges.

Analysis

Though Cardoza, the producer, knew the two sides were looking for different components of the oranges, Dr Jones and Dr Roland uncovered this fact for themselves when they talked to each other directly. The solution emerged only when one side asked the other, 'What do you want?' or 'How can I help you?'

For a successful negotiation to close the festering dispute, be the first to ask the question.

The Negotiation Process

Stage 1: Gather Full Facts

a. First, the team and its leader must be identified to handle the negotiation. The team should include all experts dealing with various aspects of the issue. The experts should identify their backups to represent them in case they are unavailable.

b. Second, information/data on the issue should be collected through research and meetings with all the stakeholders and decision-makers. Nothing should be assumed or prejudged to prevent bias.

   Also, gather intelligence about the other side—the organisation, the management, the employees—their market reputation, strengths, weaknesses, values, culture, working style, etc. The leader should hold this information confidential and share it on a need-to-know basis.

c. Third, put together a structured note containing the full facts, including the strengths, weaknesses, limitations, and expectations. Distinguish between 'needs' and 'wants' to identify gaps and areas where additional information is required.

Stage 2: Possible Solutions

1. The team to identify:
   a. Information that is yet to be collected.
   b. Information that is required from the other side.
   c. Possible scenarios with pros and cons.
   d. The areas where the other side's case is more substantial. Accepting it immediately would save both

sides time and resources, apart from maintaining the relationship.

e. The consequences for both sides if the negotiations do not succeed.

2. Present the final note, in writing, to the Management for formal clearance, specifically the bottom line.
3. Now, you are ready to forward a formal communication to the other side, defining the negotiation issues and laying down their contours. Request that the other side forward their case along similar lines.
4. Review the reply received from the other side and revise your notes. If necessary, you may contact management again to obtain fresh directives.
5. Once the brief is ready, meet with the team to check for errors. Members should refrain from sharing information about the negotiations with unauthorised persons.
6. Identify each member's role. The leader and the core members will directly engage in the negotiations, while others will convey their views to this core group. This approach ensures that the entire team speaks with one voice.
7. During the negotiations, all members should be attentive, avoiding distractions such as phone calls and messages, and focus on listening and noting non-verbal cues.
8. In the first meeting, both sides make formal statements detailing facts and their expectations. Divide the issues into three parts:
   - Identify areas in which both sides agree.
   - The areas where you need more information.
   - The areas of disagreement.

9. The negotiation process comprises several rounds of discussions, offers and counteroffers. Communicate directly, specifically, firmly, effectively, and clearly to find a positive outcome without wasting precious time. Support oral submissions with written communications to minimise confusion and misunderstandings.
10. Finalise the negotiations, duly approved by respective managements, as quickly as possible.
11. Formalise successful negotiations with a written contract carefully drafted in consultation with each other to ensure clarity during implementation, the role of each party and the timelines.

Critical skills required for handling effective negotiations are:

- Always be persuasive and diplomatic, adhering to Kautilya's principles of Saam, Daam, Dand, and Bhed.
- Be professional, control your emotions, maintain a positive environment, and respect your opponents. Losing control would hamper the logical approach.
- Be an active listener with immense patience. Listening allows one to understand what the other party said or did not say.
- Providing informative feedback to the other side is essential, but criticism must be put across gently, not directly. Sarcasm should be avoided.
- Instead of an emphatic no, offering choices (preferably more than one) will go a long way. Remember, it is not a problem for one side but for both.
- The ability to identify the interests of both sides, flexibility, diplomacy, and persuasion will go a long way in building and preserving relationships.

- Your problem-solving, creative, and analytical skills demonstrate the ability to see the issues clearly.
- Use verbal and non-verbal influencing styles. Handle negotiations assertively, occasionally using a submissive or aggressive style.
- Keeping detailed notes by all team members will help create a cohesive approach and reach the desired outcome quickly.
- Take breaks when no progress is being made in the discussions. Frequently consult with all team members, especially with the experts, so that every vital point or aspect is handled.

To get the best results in a negotiation, it is vital to identify a Win-Win approach to obtain long-term benefits. You offer help, listen attentively, and join the other side in finding a fair solution. The idea is not to prove the other side wrong but to operate in an empathetic environment in the cause of fair play, equity, and justice.

This approach eliminates distrust in the relationship. The best negotiation outcome is that both continue to work together, whatever the outcome.

The most significant advantage of taking this route—against litigation or arbitration—is considerable time, effort, and resource savings.

26

Communication in Questioning

Questioning is an essential yet powerful skill that has propelled mankind's progress. Before we finish explaining why the grass is green and the sky is blue, our children are ready to inquire into the deepest mysteries of life, the mind, space, and time. The principle of gravity might not have been discovered had Newton not asked why apples fall to the earth. The desire to question is innate and needs to be nurtured from early childhood.

Questions provide unique frameworks for thinking, which can unlock doors to unexpected revelations. They allow us to explore an issue, idea, or something unknown, developing insight as we pursue thoughts in different directions. Questions fill the information gaps, clarify points, test knowledge, and address difficulties. They are tools that compel us to rethink and challenge existing orders. The art and science of asking questions form the foundation of all knowledge.

From science to management to democracy, there is no substitute for questioning. It is fundamental to successful communication, making conversations more engaging when questions are asked. This activity aids effective teaching by boosting student engagement, learning, creativity, and curiosity, while also promoting critical thinking.

The bottom line is to never stop questioning.

Characteristics of a Good Question

The question must possess specific characteristics: it should be natural, stimulating, relevant, purposeful, clear, concise, single-dimensional, and audience-focused.

Varieties of Questions

- *Closed*: To elicit a single word, very short, or a straightforward factual answer.
- *Open*: To obtain a more detailed response regarding understanding, opinion, or feelings about what, why, and how.
- *Funnel*: To extract more details gradually, prompting memories or deeper thinking.
- *Probing*: To gain additional clarity or details.
- *Rhetorical*: To encourage reflective thinking persuasively.
- *Leading*: Designed to guide the respondent towards a desired positive or negative outcome.

Benefits of Questioning

Gathering information is a primary human activity. We use information to learn, solve problems, and understand each other more clearly. Questioning taps into the power of the mind and enriches the human experience, allowing us to analyse concepts or situations and ask relevant questions to understand various aspects of our life journey.

The benefits of asking questions include:

- Enhancing learning efficiency and scientific inquiry.

- Increasing awareness of knowledge—what we already know and how much there is to learn.
- Promoting critical thinking, which enables us to analyse our thoughts, decisions, and beliefs thereby fuelling innovation.
- Heightening awareness of our environment and broadening our perspectives.
- Reflecting a likeable trait of curiosity and intelligence, which fuels creativity, enhances happiness, drives positivity, and helps avoid stereotyping.
- Promoting communication between two minds, thereby enhancing friendship and intimacy.
- Building confidence and supporting decision-making.
- Cultivating leadership skills by fostering a lifelong learning mindset through questioning.

Questioning Skills

Questions arise from ignorance or the need to verify our knowledge. Once we ask a question, the answers will follow.

Questioning is not a simple skill; it requires reflection, perseverance, and a healthy dose of humility. To hone our questioning skills, we need to focus on:

- Considering possible answers before asking the question.
- Paying attention to the timing of our questions.
- Asking a different question or altering our approach if the information provided is incomplete or seemingly incorrect.
- Using appropriate language, structure, speed, voice, tone, style, and pauses.

The art of asking questions emerges from practice and experience, helping us overcome fears, shyness, or concerns about how others might judge our questions.

27

Communication in Marketing

You create a product or design a service (the offering) that addresses a consumer need. Your next effort is to increase its sales consistently and shorten the sales cycle. To address the competition, you must create preference—a long-term endeavour to position your offering or company in the market.

This process is known as marketing communication, which encompasses the messages you create and the media you employ. It includes branding, advertising, printed materials, packaging, online presence, public relations activities, sales presentations, sponsorships, trade show appearances, and more.

Branding

The key to marketing is the branding of the product or services. Branding encompasses the big picture that influences market share and profitability, thus providing long-term value for the company. To make a brand memorable in the minds of consumers, one must appeal to their emotions and associations, while understanding their behaviour and interests. For instance, we associate Nike with being 'sporty', 'athletic', and 'competitive', or McDonald's with 'fast food', 'affordable', and "convenient".

Branding creates a unique selling proposition (USP), differentiating the brand from competitors. A name, logo, and slogan that represent the values, personality, vision, and purpose of the offering are crucial. Apple's brand communication highlights its USP of being innovative, cutting-edge, and user-friendly, making it one of the most valuable brands globally.

The USP enables a brand to reach its target audience and raise awareness of its existence and offerings in a crowded market. Effective communication is key to conveying the brand's message and resonating with a broader audience, aiming to create memorable, positive, and lasting impressions while building strong relationships.

Another critical aspect of communication in branding is storytelling. Humans are inherently wired to respond to stories, and brands leverage this to their advantage. Storytelling allows brands to connect more deeply with consumers by appealing to their emotions and values, fostering brand loyalty and advocacy. Nike's 'Just Do It' campaign exemplifies effective brand storytelling, empowering individuals to overcome challenges and push their limits.

Your positioning strategy will help create a unique tagline and logo for the brand and develop other elements of your brand identity, including the typography, colour palette, and tone of voice. Designers and copywriters utilise these uniformly across websites, social media, packaging, and advertising, whether digital or traditional media.

Branding also plays a pivotal role in protecting the company's reputation. In today's digital age, where information spreads quickly, brands must be vigilant about their online and offline presence and the image they project to the public. A brand that communicates with transparency, honesty, and authenticity builds trust and elicits positive emotions. Conversely, brands employing misleading or dishonest communication strategies risk damaging their reputation and losing consumer trust.

Social media has emerged as a powerful tool for brands to communicate, engage and build a loyal customer base. Brands can interact with their customers in real-time, updating offerings and promptly addressing queries, feedback, and concerns. When customers feel valued and connected to the brand, they are more likely to make repeat purchases and recommend the brand to others.

Digital platforms have become effective channels for communicating messages effectively and ensuring they reach the right audience at the right time. This requires a strong understanding of the target audience's behaviour, preferences, and media consumption habits. Market research and data analysis help brands gather valuable insights, helping them tailor their communication strategies and deliver targeted messages to their audience.

Influencers significantly impact consumer purchasing decisions and promote offerings. Though their emergence has been gradual, influencers enhance brand credibility and foster stronger relationships with audiences.

In conclusion, a well-defined communication strategy is crucial in establishing and maintaining a brand's identity, building brand awareness, and persuading consumers to purchase. This is especially critical in a highly competitive business environment, where consumer behaviour and technology are constantly evolving. Brands must constantly adapt and innovate to stay ahead of the competition and connect with their target audience.

Advertising

Advertising is integral to creating a brand and getting customers' attention. An 'ad' is a paid, public communication that promotes a product, service, or brand for a desired outcome. Essentially, it involves disseminating information about the benefits of the offering to the target audience.

Advertising entails producing and disseminating messages to persuade people to buy the offering. Its goal is to create awareness and interest, convincing potential customers to make purchases while reminding current customers to continue using the product or service. An effective advertising campaign reaches target consumers with the right message, at the right time, and through the right channel.

Clear, persuasive, and audience-centric communication is vital for any marketing campaign. In today's fast-paced and highly competitive environment, businesses invest considerable resources in advertising to differentiate themselves from competitors and achieve substantial sales.

Advertising also involves building trust and maintaining relationships with customers. Companies must understand their target audience and tailor their communication strategies to convey their value proposition effectively.

Advertisements utilise various media, including print, broadcast (TV, radio), outdoor (hoardings), product integration (products and brands promoted in films, TV, Instagram, and YouTube) and digital (display, social media, search engine, and email marketing), and public relations, among others, to generate awareness and interest in the offering.

However, branding and advertising face challenges. Consumers have become adept at filtering irrelevant and uninteresting messages. Brands must maintain consistency and control over their communication, which puts them under constant pressure to create innovative, attention-grabbing ads that can cut through the noise. A negative review or social media post can spread rapidly, damaging a brand's reputation.

Shortening the Sales Cycle

The third element in marketing efforts is shortening the sales cycle. Engage with your sales and channel partners to identify and deliver the offering to the customer. Understanding the customer's buying process provides critical insights into how to shorten the sales cycle. This is a gradual process that involves significant research, analytics, and customer education. Brand-building activities must be balanced with the sales cycle to achieve the desired outcome.

Value Addition

28

Communication in Prayers

The first prayer was made by a human being when they were exposed to the menace of fire that appeared suddenly, destroyed everything, and then disappeared. That was their first encounter with the power of the Unknown—something they could not control, decipher, or understand. With the advent of language, the Unknown was named the Supreme Power, Divine Almighty, God, Ishwar, Jesus, or Allah, among others, and was depicted, directly or indirectly through humans, avatars, idols, or books.

In our prayers, we usually seek remedies for our troubles, illnesses, accidents, or financial or relationship issues. We might also ask for favours—more income, a bigger house, or a better car. Prayers can also express gratitude for the wishes already granted or for keeping us happy. With sincerity and enthusiasm, we offer special prayers seeking divine intervention when starting a new venture or journey, or before an examination or interview. Generally, our prayers are proactive, seeking blessings.

Prayers make us more comfortable with ourselves and our 'present.' They tend to enhance our confidence in addressing the issues or goals we aim to achieve. Thus, prayers to the Supreme Power become a dialogue with this "Other Me" and can be seen as a form of communication. Our wishes may or may not be fulfilled through prayers, but one outcome is certain—we gain confidence that the Supreme Power is supporting us and will help.

If help is not provided or our wishes are not granted, our faith in the Power is not diminished. We firmly believe our prayers were unanswered because we did not pray with enough fervour and complete faith. The Almighty remains our well-wisher and will help us at the appropriate time. So, we continue praying with vigour and confidence. This approach helps people spend more time being happy than sad.

However, our minds work in strange ways. We tend to remember terrible incidents, interactions, or accidents more than the time we spend being happy. Everyone notices the ink dot on a shirt pocket, but not the quality of the shirt itself.

Prayers are communicated silently or loudly, alone or in groups, while sitting in one place, walking, or travelling—whether at home, in temples, churches, gurdwaras, synagogues, or mosques. Different processes are used to pray: a word like Aum, Allah, or Jesus; a mantra; namaaz; discourses; bhajans, hymns, kirtan, or any other familiar form. Prayers offered in groups and spoken loudly tend to improve focus and bring out fervour.

Communication is also involved in celebrating a marriage, when well-wishers seek Supreme Power's blessings for the couple and their families. Similarly, it occurs at a funeral, where people seek Super Power's blessings to support the bereaved family.

29

Communication in Storytelling

Storytelling is a mode of communication that affects the listener emotionally.

Indians have used storytelling from ancient times to educate and pass on knowledge, using engaging narratives in exciting, entertaining, and creative ways to inspire audiences towards specific actions. Training sessions or speeches become more enjoyable when they incorporate a couple of stories, preferably drawn from real-life experiences.

Storytelling is also highly effective in achieving business goals and connecting with audiences in a unique way. Stories used in marketing campaigns, branding, or fundraising efforts help businesses grow.

To effectively reach an audience, a story should include the following components:

1. *The Purpose*: The best stories aim to inform, entertain, or persuade. Determining the story's purpose helps guide its structure.

2. *Structure*: A clear beginning, middle, and end make the story easier to follow and enjoy. A well-set description establishes the context, characters, and setting to engage the audience.
3. *Connection*: The story will be compelling if it resonates with the audience's feelings and experiences.
4. *Likeable Characters*: Engaging stories feature main characters with positive, relatable qualities.
5. *Emotional Appeal*: Appealing to the audience's six primary emotions—happiness, anger, sadness, fear, surprise, and disgust—helps make a story feel authentic, as emotions are powerful motivators that inspire actions.
6. *Surprises*: A story with a surprise element engages the audience more easily, with suspense or unexpected twists.
7. *Challenges*: To make them more intriguing, great stories often have conflicts or challenges for the characters to overcome.
8. *Information*: Essential details like time, location, characters, and motivations help orient the audience. Identify the problem and, if appropriate, encourage the audience to solve it for themselves. Where they are unable to find a solution, provide one for a happy ending.
9. *Personal Experiences*: Drawing on your own experiences can make a story feel more authentic and inspiring. You can also modify it as needed to better connect with the audience.

The Format

Keep the story simple and concise; adding too many details may kill the audience's interest.

Honesty and authenticity help establish the story's credibility and your authority as a storyteller. Using personal experiences adds to authenticity, while research can ensure realism and believability.

Focus on elements that enhance the listener's life and deliver an engaging, entertaining experience.

Universal themes also broaden the story's appeal.

Storytelling Skills

Effective storytelling starts with selecting the right story for the occasion and audience.

Strong verbal communication and language skills are essential. Articulation is critical to delivering the story perfectly.

Exceptional storytellers use actions to convey emotions and character traits, drawing the audience without directly explaining everything. This technique helps keep the story engaging and exciting.

Adaptability is also useful, helping adjust the story to align with the audience's desires or mood.

Practice is key to mastering storytelling; rehearse your story multiple times to internalise it and convey passion. Practising in front of a mirror, family, or friends helps build confidence and hone the techniques needed to connect emotionally with the audience. Storytelling is more complex than a public speech—missing a fact, cue, pause, or moment of intensity can make the story flat.

30

Communication in Gossip

We often equate gossip with harmful conversation, malicious rumours, or the eager spread of sensational news. Societies have traditionally viewed it as trivial, hurtful, unproductive, and, in some religions, even as a grievous sin.

However, as many of us have experienced, gossip sessions can be a way to let off steam, offering a relaxing reprieve that soothes the body and mind. Gossip can reinforce–or discourage the absence of–values, morality, and accountability. By "weeding out" problematic behaviour, gossip can encourage individuals to be less selfish and promote harmonious interaction.

Good or bad, gossip is an engine that keeps the world buzzing, whether at home, in the office, the board room, locker rooms, barber shops, salons, kitchens, or on social media. All genders, ages, professions, and financial backgrounds engage in gossip. Idle talk or casual conversations about other people's private matters, particularly those not present, are generally accepted socially.

The cross-cultural phenomenon of gossip underscores its evolutionary nature. Conversations that share experiences and perspectives from friendships and, ultimately, communities. We gossip to feel liked and accepted, to stave off loneliness, and to distract from life's challenges. So, go ahead and keep gossiping—it can be fun!

The Social Skill

Gossip, often wielded with surprising social power, has intrigued psychologists, social scientists, and management experts alike. Generally, people gossip more when focusing on others rather than on themselves.

Research suggests that gossip is a well-developed social skill tied to strategies that men and women use in finding compatible partners.

Studies show that women are more inclined than men to gossip, particularly to disparage potential rivals. In a study, the female participants spent 67 per cent of their conversation time gossiping, compared to 55 per cent among male participants, often focusing on topics like physical appearance, fashion, relationships, TV shows, celebrities, and children.

For women, gossiping can be a bonding mechanism, albeit sometimes tinged with negativity—a key element in female friendships. From a young age, girls learn that showing interest in friends' lives creates closeness, a sense of connection, and the reassurance of mutual care.

Over time, this behaviour helps women build more resilient social networks. It can also prepare them for later life stages, especially as women tend to outlive men and may spend a longer period without their partners.

Men also gossip, though it often goes unlabelled, viewed instead as networking, venting, or keeping in touch. Popular topics include secrets, romantic interests, sports, scandals, promotions, salary changes, office politics, cars and the latest gadgets. To impress others, men tend to focus on wealth, athleticism, and superiority. Shorter attention spans at work mean men may take frequent breaks, leading to extended gossip sessions.

Both genders. However, participate in and are subject to gossip, particularly about relationships. In typical exchanges, one person may disparage another by criticising their character, appearance, or actions. Extroverts, being more inclined to engage and converse, may gossip more frequently than their introverted counterparts.

The Workplace

At the workplace, gossip can take a different dimension. Light-hearted gossip over coffee may relieve the stress and monotony of working long hours on challenging, time-bound projects. Many office-going professionals admit to gossiping at work, which often serves as a primary source of information on workplace happenings and socially acceptable organisational behaviour. Informal networks, such as the grapevine, provide insights into the 'pulse' of an organisation. When used judiciously, these networks can be powerful tools for gathering information.

Some people may exploit gossip to enhance their own status, power, or prestige, or even as a tactic to undermine colleagues with remarks like, 'He always takes long lunches,' or, 'That is just how she is.' Although gossip cannot be eliminated, its negative effects can be mitigated. Setting clear policies and expectations about workplace behaviour can help.

While gossip can foster bonds, trust, and friendships within teams, especially for millennials, its risks should not be ignored. For instance, spreading misinformation or rumours can create a hostile environment, erode morale, and even drive attrition.

With open and transparent communication, leaders can help employees feel informed, reducing the need for them to seek updates informally. Since gossip can often outpace formal communication methods, such as emails or messages, it can be an asset when managed constructively.

Consequences of Workplace Gossip

Negative workplace gossip can have several adverse effects:

- Loss of productivity and wasted time.
- Increased jealousy, anxiety, and mistrust, leading to a toxic atmosphere and low morale.
- Divisiveness as employees take sides.
- Damaged reputations and hurt feelings.
- Higher attrition, as good employees may leave due to a negative and unhealthy work atmosphere.
- Limited career progression for gossipers, as they may be viewed as unprofessional.

31

Communication in Honking

Crorepati options seen on the back of a three-wheeler:

As the red light turns green, blowing my car horn will:	
Make the cars ahead vanish into thin air.	Widen the road.
Give my car wings to fly.	All/None of the above.

It all started in Kolkata, where the joke has always been that one must use the horn to drive, as nobody listens otherwise. Over time, this habit spread to cities across India, with Delhi becoming the worst.

We love honking—it has become an inseparable part of our culture. Every coach in state-licensed driving schools insists the learners use the horn liberally—honking even before starting the engine!

The horn also serves as a display of power, asserting a right of way. We honk at cars, rickshaw pullers, and even pedestrians. A traffic jam becomes a cacophony: horns from buses, cars, motorcycles, and e-rickshaws—each trying to get ahead and getting nowhere. Once, a motorcyclist was caught on CCTV honking at a speed breaker, despite the roads being empty at 5 in the morning!

The 'blink-of-an-eye' delay before honking starts as traffic lights turn green has been described by Wikipedia as a 'nanosecond.' India is perhaps the only country that encourages this practice—most trucks and buses display 'Horn Please' in bold, colourful paint on their backs.

We all have our own codes: for using the horn, for overtaking from right, overtaking from left, warning the driver in front for going too slow, for keeping me alive even though I'm driving dangerously. Turning right even though I have signalled for left, and so on. The codes use long horns, toots, and spaces in between in different combinations.

The only issue is that the meaning of each code is known only to the driver who is honking at that time. So, the chances of the listeners deciphering the purpose of the horn used on their left, right, behind, far, or near are remote, if not impossible, particularly when they have no clue about the source.

It's high time a programmer devises a language that could be applied nationally and with humour.

32

Communication in Humour

Humour is a universal phenomenon found in most cultures and is a form of communication that elicits smiles, amusement, merriment, or laughter. A hearty laugh lightens our stressed minds, putting us in a positive frame of mind. Humour may come from something seen, heard, or imagined—like a witty line, a playful tease, a thought, a one-liner or a funny story. Everyone loves humour.

Humour explores the absurdity in situations, allowing people to laugh even through a crisis. It is an emotion that surfaces unconsciously, allowing people to release suppressed aggressive and instinctual urges in socially acceptable ways. Humour offers relief from tensions arising from people's desires or fears, serving as a defence against adverse real-life situations and emotional consequences.

From its light-hearted forms to its more absurd expressions, humour can play an instrumental role in fostering camaraderie, building social bonds, or even attracting a mate. Humour, the ability to express or perceive what is funny, serves as both a source of entertainment and an effective way to cope with awkward or stressful situations. The release of the nervous energy produces laughter and delight.

Humour often follows a pattern rooted in emotional dynamics, which infuses situations with life and elicits laughter, giggles, or smirks. Laughter acts as a release mechanism, where a sudden stimulus can trigger the outpouring of stored emotions from various sources. For example, the hearty laughter of a group of schoolboys at a minor incident often reflects their pent-up frustration with a monotonous lesson.

What Makes Us Laugh?

With such a diverse range of functions and styles, humour manifests in countless variations. But why do some jokes make us laugh while others fall flat?

Scientists offer different explanations for why some things are funnier than others, yet they all agree that humour often hinges on the disruption of expectations.

Broadly, humour occurs when three conditions are met:

- Something challenges one's perception of how the world 'ought to be'.
- The challenge seems benign, and
- A person perceives both interpretations simultaneously.

In other words, something is funny when it appears absurd or even slightly threatening but is essentially harmless—as when a comedian says something shocking but unserious. Humour arises from recognising how incongruent details fit together or when a paradox exists between expectations and outcomes.

Humour frequently includes an unexpected, often sudden, shift in perspective—moving from seriousness to playfulness. It arises from the brain's capacity to recognise errors within belief structures, identifying faulty reasoning. Or humour might emerge when two distinct frames of reference are juxtaposed, creating an intentional collision.

Humour frequently includes an unexpected, often sudden, shift in perspective—moving from seriousness to playfulness. It arises from the brain's capacity to recognise errors within belief structures, identifying faulty reasoning. Or humour might arise when two distinct frames of reference are placed side by side, creating an intentional clash.

Humour is often triggered by a punch line, which causes an audience to abruptly shift from an initial understanding to a secondary, opposing one: 'Is the doctor at home?' the patient asked in a hushed, bronchial tone. 'No,' the doctor's young and pretty wife whispered in response. 'Come right in'.

The physical presence of beer in the lower part of a glass inscribed with 'HALF EMPTY', creates a collision between two frames of reference, generating humour in that realisation. For this reason, the intonation and timing of the punch line are crucial to a joke's impact.

Jokes are funny because they catch the listener off guard, introducing an element of surprise with a twist that amuses. A ridiculous feature—whether a physical peculiarity or an embarrassing mistake—adds to the punch. Thus, humour often depends on contradiction or absurdity to provoke laughter.

People with a strong sense of humour often display qualities such as a willingness to take risks in their jokes and a keen awareness of how their humour is received. This is why humorous individuals tend to be more intelligent, and humour itself is regarded as the highest form of creativity.

Cultural factors, location, age, political orientation, taste, personal preferences, and timing all affect whether a humorous remark is deemed good, bad, or indifferent. The style and technique of the humourist define the originality, emphasis, and economy of words.

Despite its light-hearted appearance, humour is a serious business. A multi-crore industry—encompassing stand-up comedy, circus clowns, plays, movies, limericks, and comics—exists solely to entertain us.

The Benefits of Humour

1. Humour is a positive coping mechanism that enables people to face adversity, fears, and challenging situations.
2. Being able to laugh can cushion the emotional impact of difficult experiences and lighten tense atmospheres. As a shared experience, humour can strengthen bonds among friends and family. For romantic partners, it often brings out the best in each other, bringing them close together.

In the workplace, humour can:

- Build stronger relationships within teams and improve camaraderie between colleagues.
- Relieve boredom.
- Create a positive environment.
- Break down communication barriers and ease the tone of directives or requests made to colleagues.
- Boost productivity and team cohesion.
- Stabilise group dynamics during times of crisis.

Anyone Can Cultivate Humour

To start incorporating humour:

- Maintain a positive outlook in all situations.
- Love humanity, love yourself.

- Accept yourself as you are unconditionally—you were born to be great!
- Accept others the way they are.
- Take it easy; life is beautiful.
- Ignore insults and forgive your critics.
- Like any other creative process, humour will come unexpectedly.
- Enjoy life—become a humourist!

33

Communication in Anger

Anger is a complex, commonly experienced emotion that can range from mild annoyance to displeasure to intense rage. We often associate anger with negative outcomes, as it can harm both the initiator and the responder. Shouting places us in a negative mode, triggering a defence mechanism that activates a fight, flight or freeze response. This reaction increases cortisol and adrenalin levels, disturbing the body's balance. As a result, we may make poor decisions, leading to physical and mental issues.

Anger often arises when we believe or perceive that someone has wronged us—whether physically, mentally, or socially—unfairly, unjustly, or deliberately. When our ego is threatened, we may feel compelled to assert ourselves. We may shout to discipline others or feel helpless and act irrationally in response to a perceived insult or an offence against someone we care about.

In nearly all societies and religions, anger is seen as problematic, even sinful, as it damages relationships—both personal and professional—and diminishes quality of life. Rather than behaving rationally and proactively, we become slaves to our reactionary behaviour, so absorbed in blaming others that we stop thinking logically, going against all the values, and learnings we have absorbed.

Have you ever wondered why we start shouting when we are angry?

Once, a Wise man was bathing with his disciples by the riverbank when a fight erupted nearby. It began with an argument between two bathers nearby and quickly escalated to shouting.

The Wise man asked, 'Why do people start shouting in anger even though they are standing next to each other?'

The disciples were clueless.

The Wise man explained, 'In an angry match, the distance between the hearts of the two persons increases. They start speaking loudly to cover this distance.'

He concluded, 'People speak softly when their hearts are close—just like lovers.'

Occasionally, we indulge in angry exchanges without any reason. A common example is road rage when a car accident occurs. Instead of waiting to assess fault, we may immediately react, shouting, and using foul language. Why not listen calmly and allow the other person to explain? Why not speak civility, in a measured tone? Why should a minor scratch on a fully insured car provoke such an intense reaction?

We may not realise that anger rarely guarantees a desired outcome, and frequent anger is detrimental to relationships. Shouting at children is as harmful as physical punishment, leaving them with lasting anxiety and restlessness that can hamper their physical and mental growth.

However, not all anger or provocation is harmful. In some cases, it can lead to positive actions like protecting oneself, changing attitudes, or solving problems. Adrenaline can motivate protective actions or drive change if anger is channelled constructively. In certain cases, feigned anger, as seen when a young mother playfully scolds her child, can be harmless.

> There is a science behind communication in anger. When we perceive an insult, there is a split-second gap before our mind registers it as such. Anger, as a response, is reactive and temporarily numbs logical thought. If we stay in that moment, anger persists; however, if we allow the moment to pass, reason takes over, allowing us to reflect on the situation objectively. With time, the perceived insult may seem trivial or even inspire corrective action.

The Russian philosopher George Gurdjieff shared advice from his father, who, on his deathbed, said to him, 'Gurdjieff, whenever you feel angry, never reply before 24 hours have passed.' Gurdjieff credits this advice for his spiritual journey.

Similarly, the famous US investment banker JP Morgan would remain silent during meetings. On one occasion, a competitor entered his office and unleashed a barrage of abuses while Morgan was facing the other side. Once the competitor was exhausted and sat down in a chair, Morgan turned around his chair and calmly asked, 'Sir, could you please repeat the abuses?' The abuser was speechless.

Abusing someone is like vomiting; once expelled, there is no poison left.

Guru Nanak gives another perspective on anger management with these words:

एक ने कही, दूसरे ने मानी, नानक कहे दोनों ही ज्ञानी।
एक ने कही, दूसरे ने ना मानी, नानक कहे दोनो ही अज्ञानी।

(Guru Nanak says that if one person makes a request and the other agrees, both are wise. If there is a disagreement, both are unwise.)

To manage anger constructively, consider these strategies:

- *Acknowledge its existence*: Denial will only make management more challenging.
- *Think before speaking; respond, do not react*: Pause to gather your thoughts before saying something you might regret, which also allows others time to reflect.
- *Identify triggers*: Analyse what makes you angry. Is it due to a specific event, decision, or person? Are you feeling threatened or scared?
- *Take a break*: Engage in physical or mental activity to reduce the stress, allowing you to return to the issue with a calmer perspective.
- *Express concerns calmly*: Once composed, communicate your needs respectfully and directly. Address the issue, not the person.
- *Avoid sarcasm*: Be assertive instead.
- *Do not hold a grudge; forgive*: Holding onto resentment can cloud positive feelings and ultimately leave you bitter. Forgiving helps you learn from the situation, remain positive, and strengthen your relationship.
- *Practice relaxation techniques*: The daily moments you reserve for yourself—your 'me time' of physical exercise, yoga, music, or meditation, can help address anger over time.
- *Seek help if necessary*: It is always good to seek help when required. Suppressing anger for a long can lead to serious health issues.

34

Value-Based Communication

When we think of value-based communication, a 'shlok' from ancient text comes to mind:

> सत्यं ब्रूयात् प्रियं ब्रूयात्, न ब्रूयात् सत्यम् अप्रियम्।
> प्रियं च नानृतम् ब्रूयात्, एष धर्मः सनातनः॥
>
> (सत्य बोलना चाहिये, प्रिय बोलना चाहिये, पर अप्रिय सत्य नहीं बोलना चाहिये और प्रिय असत्य भी नहीं बोलना चाहिये। यही सनातन धर्म है।)
>
> Speak the truth; speak pleasant (or good thoughts). But avoid conveying unpleasant truths or pleasant lies; this is the way of life.

These observations reflect our beliefs and values. We must be honest but avoid communication that would hurt the listener—whether intentional or not. For instance, referring to a person with one leg as 'lame' would undoubtedly hurt him; describing him as Differently Abled would convey empathy, aligning with our values. Empathy in everyday conversation demonstrates sensitivity toward respect for human beings, commitment to values we hold close to heart, and consideration for the environment.

David Domke, communication scholar, author, and political consultant, aptly put it: 'Value Communication' is the 'glue that holds social movements together'. Mahatma Gandhi, Abraham Lincoln, and Martin Luther King built powerful movements by uniting diverse groups of people through shared values. Our communication strategies should, therefore, reflect the values we uphold.

Value-based communication, grounded in shared values, is essential to:

- Lend authenticity to our words.
- Ensure they are received positively and remembered.
- Connect with people easily, foster positivity and build consensus.
- Resonate with the values in our hearts and minds, encouraging everyone to communicate impactfully.
- Empower us with wisdom, making us WISER.

35

Conscious Communication

When we talk of conscious communication, the first thing that comes to mind are words ascribed to Socrates:

> Before you speak, ask yourself if what you will say is true, kind, necessary, and helpful?

It takes a couple of years to learn to speak, but it takes a lifetime to know what to say, when to say it, and how to say it. Although we talk about many things throughout the day, do we take a moment to think and analyse before each utterance?

Purpose

Communication is at the heart of all our relationships, professional and personal. A conscious communicator must know the purpose of the communication—even if it is only for amusement. Thus, the purpose of conscious communication is to nurture and sustain our connection with others. A lack of purpose reflects an empty mind or lack of mental application. Speaking to the point and with precision makes for an enjoyable conversation, more likely leading to the desired outcome.

Generous Soul

Communication is a vast ocean of language, signs, symbols, gestures, expressions, tone, body language, emotions, and even energy flow. Our eyes tell countless stories and even silence can convey a powerful message. Often, our emotions reveal more than our words can express. A child, for example, communicates a range of emotions without speaking—her love and compassion overflow through her body language.

We quickly understand a child's communication because her pure heart reflects a generous soul, free of hidden agendas, misunderstandings, or conflict. A gracious soul radiates positivity and optimism, helping to build and nurture connections.

Meditation helps us to know ourselves more deeply, aligning us with our compassionate souls. It prepares us to listen with tolerance, see with compassion, and speak with love, turning us into generous souls.

Active Listening

Contrary to general perception, for a conscious communicator, listening skills are more important than speaking skills. We enjoy talking—to impress, build and sustain relationships. However, your words will not achieve their aim if the listener is preoccupied with preparing a reply instead of genuinely responding. Such a listener hears but does not listen. That is why we appreciate conversing with a good listener. Be a conscious communicator who listens patiently, attentively, and without prejudice.

Accountability

A conscious communicator takes care and responsibility to ensure their words do not hurt the listener's sentiments or feelings. This approach arises from self-love, allowing the communicator to extend that same compassion to others. They listen to understand and communicate authentically and consciously.

Speak Softly & Calmly

Speaking in a soft tone and calm manner creates a sense of safety, keeping the connection space open and making others comfortable with our communication.

Brevity

Using short sentences and speaking to the point engages others more effectively.

Response

A response is proactive and constructive, fostering a calm and healthy discussion. In contrast, a reaction is impulsive, aggressive, and often rooted in emotional outbursts.

Pauses

Conscious communication involves not only the art of sharing but also of receiving. Allowing a pause after sharing a thought gives others the space to absorb and process what you have said. It also helps the speaker become aware of how their communication impacts the listener.

36

The Power of Communication

Communication connects us universally in all spheres of life. This powerful medium builds effective relationships, helps us achieve desired results, and enhances the quality of our lives. It allows us to lead meaningful and satisfying lives—physically and emotionally.

Communication is the essence of life, enabling us to express feelings, convey information, make requests, and share ideas, thoughts, experiences, and needs. It serves six primary purposes: *inform*, *ask*, *express feelings*, *imagine*, *influence*, and *meet social expectations*. Communication avoids confusion by minimising misunderstandings and optimising time. It resolves or prevents problems and conflicts, builds relationships, trust, and teamwork, and fosters collaboration, ultimately leading to enhanced outcomes.

The powers of communication can be categorised as follows:

Information Exchange

The genesis of communication lay in the need to warn each other of impending dangers and offer help. At its core, communication is the exchange of information between two or more people.

Initially, messages were exchanged non-verbally. Later, with the invention of language and writing, verbal and written elements were incorporated. The range of communication was initially limited by the reach of one's voice, but as methods evolved, tools like writing and postal systems expanded this range. A quantum leap occurred with the advent of digital communication, which, with the internet, now transmits information over vast distances at extraordinary speed.

Data and information have been codified and developed into knowledge in diverse fields. Knowledge contributes to personal growth through new skills, cultural awareness, and broadened perspectives. It helps in decision-making, problem-solving, and innovation. Knowledge and information are essential to the economic well-being of society, contributing to stability and sustainable development globally.

Relationships

The most direct and significant benefit of information exchange is its role in building relationships, shaped by the way people interact with each other, both physically and emotionally. The concept of family emerged from these connections, eventually leading to the formation of societies. These developments helped cultivate culture, which varies regionally, influenced by terrain and climate. The need for governance subsequently gave rise to political structures.

Advancements in agriculture, industry, technology, and the internet have deepened human interdependence. Open communication is the most significant factor in fostering care, trust, affection, mutual respect, commitment, and honesty in relationships. Healthy relationships increase one's sense of worth, confidence, and belonging, contributing to a happier and more fulfilled life. We are empowered to learn more about ourselves and innovate.

Influencing

Perhaps the most remarkable power of communication lies in its ability to evoke emotions in others. Emotions, whether positive or negative—love, hate, joy, or distress—can all be induced through skilful communication.

Emotions can inspire courageous or destructive behaviours. Love, the most profound of these emotions, is especially powerful, as seen in the bond between mother and child or between a couple.

The power to influence, often in subtle or intangible ways, has shaped hierarchical structures in the chain of command. Managers or leaders utilise this power extensively to inspire others to deliver excellent results, encouraging them to think, grow, and accomplish goals.

Lasting results are often achieved when influence is exercised without formal authority. In such cases, the leader paints an inspiring picture of the future for those they wish to motivate. Yet, this requires effort. One must identify preferred influencing and inspirational styles, using them with an open mind, active listening, and a curious approach.

37

Smart Communication

ऐसी वाणी बोलिए मन का आप खोए।
औरन को शीतल करे, आपहुं शीतल होए॥

—कबीर दास

(हमेशा ऐसी भाषा बोलने चाहिए जो सामने वाले को सुनने से अच्छा लगे। उन्हें सुख की अनुभूति हो और खुद को भी आनंद का अनुभव हो।)

Speak humbly to make a conversation an enjoyable activity, both for the speaker and the listener.

Communication skills involve listening, speaking, and observing impact and effectiveness while attempting to achieve the goals of a conversation. Selecting words is essential, but how you deliver—energy, pronunciation, pitch, loudness, and tone—is more relevant. We may need to convey an offensive message, but the delivery should always be subtle.

Similarly, we may have to convey sad news, but the delivery should be empathetic.

To be a successful communicator and build positive relationships in personal, corporate, or business life:

- Keep working on Active Listening, Active Watching, Active Reading, and Active Writing. Be alert and listen with patience and empathy to be a conversationalist in demand.
- Be a LISTENER, and you will always win an argument, negotiation, or bargain. The Dalai Lama once said, 'If I am only speaking, I am repeating what I know. But if I am listening, I am always learning something new. This means humility and vulnerability.'
- Be relaxed, friendly and careful while speaking. Before you let the words escape, reflect.
- Simple, clear, concise, coherent, and courteous language in your written and spoken messages will win friends.
- Take time to enunciate and articulate every word to increase the listener's comfort level. Your clarity will improve.
- Dealing with a client assertively ensures you never have to worry about conflict, and you can say NO easily. It means explaining the reasons for your stand firmly.
- Open and transparent communication is the key to building winning teams. *Train your people so well that they leave you, but treat your people so well that they do not want to leave you!*
- If you want to become a great conversationalist and gain admirers, follow these simple pointers:
    - Non-verbal cues—smiling and open gestures—convey your open-mindedness and positivity.

- Enjoy the experience of a good interaction. Avoid scoring points.
- Never be in a hurry, whatever the provocation (excluding emergencies). Maintain eye contact, and you will manifest confidence.
- When you meet a person, mentally note five things that impress you the most. Ask questions on these points to bring out their strengths and encourage conversation. Your reputation as a great conversationalist will grow phenomenally.
- Avoid mentioning those things that you did not like about them.
- Show respect by allowing others to speak first and by speaking in their language. Identifying when to speak and when to keep silent makes a maximum impact.
- Allow natural silences to occur when talking. Give the other person time to process new information and respond comfortably.
- A storytelling structure can help your message land more effectively, entertainingly, and engagingly.
- Stay on course: Keep track of the objective of your conversation and return to it if the discussion wanders off.
- Get feedback to consistently improve your communication skills. Ask your listeners if you are being clear or if you should repeat yourself.

The Bonus

38

Communication in Music

Initially, there was noise. Crickets created melody, birds brought variety, and music was finally born when a young mother crooned a lullaby to make her baby sleep and catch a nap herself. This is how babies recognise rhythms, intervals, sounds, and the acoustic properties of syllables and melodies in language. Young children's communication journey starts with singing songs to music, helping them to expand their vocabulary and memory. Each one of us has music in our blood.

Music has been a communication medium since ancient times. From tribal chants and folk songs to orchestral compositions, it has played a significant role in religious and cultural ceremonies, conveying messages, beliefs, and culture, and preserving traditions. This universal language connects people across communities, backgrounds, generations, ages, religions, and cultures. In a world full of strife, it breaks down barriers and fosters diversity, inclusivity, understanding and empathy.

One of the most intriguing qualities of music is its power to evoke strong emotions and resonate deeply with individuals. Whether it is the stirring melody of a classical composition, the infectious beat of a pop song, or the soulful lyrics of a bhajan, music's expressive qualities convey thoughts and ideas that connect with listeners. Through self-expression in music, we can connect with our inner selves and others more deeply. Messages of love, hope, and solidarity reach our hearts and souls, leaving a lasting emotional impact.

Music has also served as a means of storytelling and passing down oral histories across generations. From Ram Lilas to modern-day music festivals, it has always played a central role in social gatherings and events, uniting people from diverse backgrounds in a shared experience of rhythm and harmony, and fostering a sense of community belonging.

Artists draw inspiration from their own experiences and culture, interpreting their emotions into melodies, rhythms, lyrics, and harmony. A slow, melancholic melody may evoke sadness, loss, or longing, while an intense and fast-paced rhythm spreads joy and energy. Harmonies that complement each other communicate happiness, relaxation, and serenity, while clashing harmonies convey excitement, anger, or unpleasantness. Instruments and vocal techniques add layers, creating a multi-dimensional experience.

Our engagement with music, whether at a live concert or through a streaming service, is driven by its ability to communicate emotion. Music can arouse strong feelings and recall memories; it can uplift us, deepen our spiritual experience, or evoke love or loss.

Musicians continue to explore and experiment across genres and styles, profoundly impacting individuals and communities. Music enhances awareness and perceptions, providing platforms for dialogue and social change. Its universality makes it a valuable communication tool, transcending cultural, societal, and language barriers. Compositions like *Vande Mataram* united the nation against the British and continue to serve as anthems for unity, peace, and prosperity.

Playing or listening to music (naad) is entertaining and therapeutic. It helps individuals express and process their emotions, unlock their minds' potential and enhance emotional resilience and mental well-being. Music offers catharsis, providing an outlet for emotions that are difficult to express through words. Scientists suggest that synchronised listening aligns brain rhythms and promotes social bonding, strengthening familial and social connections.

Impact of Music on Human Behaviour

Just as one does not cry in a specific language, music is not bound by language or instruments; it is rooted in human connection, allowing one to open their heart and feel.

Music serves as an excellent icebreaker, bonding families, declaring love, and creating a joyful environment for occasions such as birthdays, weddings, or festivals.

When musical instruments and the human voice work together, they create magical melodies that inspire, stimulate, or soothe the human brain. The aesthetics of music often reflect the cultural and social contexts of their times.

Musicians use their craft to convey messages, tell stories, and express their innermost thoughts and feelings. Music is the art of organising thoughts in musical expressions. It enhances anticipation, concentration, body language, sequencing, coordination, and vocabulary—traits common to verbal communication. Through melody, rhythm, and harmony, music conveys emotions and ideas in a way that people understand and appreciate universally.

Music is not just entertainment or artistic expression; it is a powerful form of communication that touches hearts, unites people, and conveys human experience beyond words. As we engage with music's sound and rhythms, let us remember how it connects us to the world around us.

Live performances offer a unique experience; a palpable collective energy fills the auditorium. The performer weaves a magical bond between the music and the audience, skilfully blending exquisite tone control, musical understanding, and raw energy. Through this artistry, music stirs profound emotions— joy, grief, and sadness—while painting vivid images of nature. It offers a sanctuary for daydreams and serves as an escape from the rigours of 'everyday life'.

However, music has also been wielded as a tool for propaganda and manipulation, resulting in societal harm and division. This underscores music's potential as a communication tool, for better or worse.

In today's digital age, music has become more accessible, reaching a global audience, and fostering cross-cultural interaction. New technology and digital tools enable greater experimentation and innovation, amplifying music's communicative power. No other medium transmits human emotions or moods as swiftly and effectively. It is no surprise that music captivates people worldwide, with 90 per cent of the world's population enjoying it!

Acknowledgements

I want to acknowledge the beautiful artwork produced by Sakshi Agarwal for the book cover. She understood the concept and created the design with finesse and elegance.

I appreciate Bidisha Srivastava's immense patience in completing the editing work. I also want to thank Manjul Publishing House for eliciting confidence in the book.

About the Authors

Anand Chhabra thinks that sharing your learning with others increases your understanding of concepts and their application in real time. But in today's fast-paced life, the way to effective sharing is in digestible bites.

Facets of Communication 360°, Anand's second book, which he has co-authored with Vinod Mitra, is on communication, which while sounding simple, can be complex when applied. Anand continues to share his experiences, examining its different facets. It is communication that drives all our activities in the entire universe. There is a topic for everyone—corporates, individuals, start-ups, and network marketers to excel in their chosen fields.

Anand Chhabra started his career as a lecturer, went on to crack the civil services, eventually turning to imparting corporate training, mentoring and coaching, but what he likes to do the most is write. His first book was *The Power of Implementation: The Missing Link between Corporate Training & Sales Target* (Beeja House, 2023). He can be contacted at anandchhabra@gmail.com.

Vinod Mitra started his career as a mining engineer in Bharat Gold Mines Ltd. (erstwhile K.G.F.), Kolar, Karnataka, and learned the benefits of discipline, analytical approach, and continuous training. In his subsequent thirty-two-year career, and twelve years of being a consultant in the public and private sector cement industry, he focused on understanding the hows and whys of delivery processes to enhance the bottom lines for organisations. He developed an interest in management skills and became a qualified coach. He also became a qualified Environmental and Earth Sciences expert.

Vinod earnestly believes, 'One is alive till he continues to learn and becomes dead once he stops learning.' He worked as a part-time lecturer and examiner in various universities to pass his learning and knowledge to the younger generation. As an examiner for the Directorate General of Mines Safety, he was later appointed as its technical advisor.

He believes communication is the most neglected or misunderstood subject, so, he readily joined hands with Anand Chhabra in sharing his experiences on communication. You can write to Vinod at vinodkmitra@gmail.com.

www.ingramcontent.com/pod-product-compliance
Lightning Source LLC
La Vergne TN
LVHW090518110826
845146LV00003B/908

* 9 7 8 9 3 5 5 4 3 7 8 4 6 *